TANU RABBANAN:
OUR RABBIS TAUGHT

Essays on the Occasion of the Centennial of the Central Conference of American Rabbis

1989 YEARBOOK
VOLUME II

Edited by Joseph B. Glaser

CENTRAL CONFERENCE OF AMERICAN RABBIS
192 LEXINGTON AVENUE
NEW YORK, N.Y. 10016

Library of Congress Catalog Card Number: 4-10495
ISBN 0-88123-012-X

Copy editing, typesetting, and publishing services provided by:
SPECIAL EDITION, P.O. Box 091097, Columbus, Ohio 43209
(614) 231-4088

PRINTED IN THE UNITED STATES OF AMERICA

THIS VOLUME HAS BEEN MADE POSSIBLE

BY A GRANT FROM THE FAMILY OF

RABBI ISRAEL BETTAN, ז"ל

1889-1957

Revered Teacher, Inspired Preacher, CCAR President

Central Conference of American Rabbis

192 Lexington Avenue

New York, N.Y. 10016

TABLE OF CONTENTS

INTRODUCTION

JOSEPH B. GLASER

So we are now 100 years old. We are bigger, in both size and function, but are we different?

We are still stretching the boundaries, still testing, still leading, still lagging, still erring, still correcting, but we are still not still.

Like our predecessors of a century ago, we still tend to alternately pontificate and posture and yet retain the ability to laugh at ourselves.

Although the *Shoah* and the establishment of the State of Israel have intervened, we have still among us those whose yearning for the actualization of *Yerushelayim shel mala* cannot tolerate the cruelly imposed realities of *Yerushelayim shel mata*.

We are yet confused as to whether the rabbinate is primarily *doing* or *being*, whether rabbinic authority is ascribed or earned, and why a rabbi can be "lonely" when surrounded by all those people. With all our worldliness and, in the case of most of us now, having been brought up in times of plenty, we still quake in the face of salary negotiations while still falling prey to the granting of favors.

Occasional critics to the contrary, the passion for social justice has not diminished in the American Reform rabbinate. In community after community members of the CCAR are engaged daily and deeply in many causes. The difference is in the rhetoric, in the style, in the type of cause alive today as opposed to those that absorbed the rabbis of decades ago.

There may be a shade of difference in the level, if not the quality, of pastoral care rendered by today's rabbi, more schooled in the insights and even the techniques of psychology and social work. But even here, it is the caring, the common sense, the mining of the treasure of Judaism that performs the service to the soul — and that, too, could not have changed.

With the enormous technological changes that have taken place — in media, communication, transportation, education, medicine — how could it be that there is nothing new under the rabbinic sun? True — the rabbi is no longer the rare college graduate in the community. True — the capacity to reach the rabbi and the capacity for rabbinic response have increased by geometric proportions, resulting in the rabbi's being spread thin quantitatively as well as qualitatively. But there are rabbis today who have the character to say "no"; who have the motivation to continue learning on a serious and sustained level; and who have the care to focus on each

1

individual person, project, or sermon — just as in the "good old days." For, in days of yore as today and tomorrow, what the rabbi *is* is what being a rabbi is all about. It's how tall you stand in the face of criticism, how trustworthy you are with confidences, how patient you are with inadequacy, how gentle you are in confrontation — yet how strong. It is how dignified and straight you are in matters of finance, how caring you are of your own family while yet, in balance, having real concern for those in your spiritual care who are in need of you — simply because you are a rabbi.

In a word, *menschlichkeit*. Or, as the sainted Leo Baeck put it to an ordination class almost 70 years ago in Germany:

> The message is not the sermon of a preacher, but the man himself. The man must be the message. The rabbi must not deliver a message. He must deliver himself.

Seventy years and over 150 women rabbis later (including Baeck's own great-granddaughter-in-law), those words epitomize the mission of the rabbi better than any others ever spoken.

Over the century, the Central Conference of American Rabbis has been committed to enhancing the capacity of the rabbi to function — and to *be* — in keeping with that goal. Although I believe that it has succeeded largely, what is important is that we ensure its capacity to do so. This requires constant analysis and vigilance in every area of concern. The essays contained in this volume, which build on the excellent histories of Sidney L. Regner, Eugene J. Lipman, and Elliot L. Stevens, seek to probe the future within that context.

We praise God for bringing us to this day. We pray God will let our successors rejoice in yet another centennial.

THE HISTORY OF THE CONFERENCE
Part I: 1889-1964

SIDNEY L. REGNER

The Central Conference of American Rabbis, the first permanent national American rabbinical organization, was established only after several prior efforts had failed. For 40 years Isaac M. Wise had been agitating for a meeting ground for rabbis. Several attempts to convene rabbinical meetings in the 1840s proved fruitless. A meeting was held in 1855 in Cleveland in response to a call signed by Wise and eight other rabbis for a gathering of ministers and delegates of congregations in order to organize a synod. Not exclusively a rabbinical conference since a few laymen also attended, it was intended to bring together Orthodox and Reform elements. Among those who attended was Isaac Leeser, the outstanding leader of American traditionalism. A statement of principles was adopted and a date set for action to be taken on a synod. But controversy over principles and compromises was aroused, and attacks by both Orthodox spokesmen and radical Reformers made any further meeting futile. Only one practical result came from this conference: its committee on prayerbook met and supported the publication of Wise's *Minhag America*.

In 1869 a conference of Reform rabbis was held in Philadelphia, and further, disconnected meetings were held in 1870 in Cleveland and New York and in 1871 in Cincinnati. Although the latter meetings were called ostensibly to revise the *Minhag America,* other business was introduced. The session in Cincinnati was actually a rabbinical conference, at which, in addition to the consideration of the prayerbook, questions of religious education were considered, the need for a seminary was pressed, and the establishment of a congregational union and synod was planned. But no permanent organization eventuated from these gatherings.

The Pittsburgh Conference of 1885, notable for its adoption of the Pittsburgh Platform which was regarded for many decades as the authoritative expression of the principles of Reform Judaism, met the same fate as had all previous rabbinical conferences. It had been planned as the first meeting of a permanent organization; however, the session called for the following year never took place.

The Rabbinical Literary Association of America, created by Max Lilienthal in 1880, held meetings simultaneously with the Union of American Hebrew Congregations (organized in 1873)

3

and was actually, except in name, a rabbinical conference, with commissions appointed to consider such subjects as a proposed synod, marriage laws, funeral rites, and other matters. The Association published *The Hebrew Review,* a quarterly containing the proceedings of the annual meetings, papers delivered at the sessions, and other essays. With the death of Lilienthal in 1882 the organization went out of existence.

There were also two regional groups of rabbis, both organized in 1885: the Conference of Southern Rabbis, and the Jewish Ministers Association composed of rabbis in the eastern part of the United States.

The failure of these early efforts to establish a permanent conference is not difficult to explain. The first attempts to unite Orthodox and Reform rabbis into one body only hardened the opposition between the two. Even the first conferences of Reform rabbis, such as that in Philadelphia in 1869, accentuated the differences between radical and moderate Reformers. Wise accounted for the failure of the early conferences in terms of the rivalry of Jews who had come from various lands, the isolation of congregations from each other and their desire to perpetuate accustomed usages, and the individualism of the rabbis. It was not until he had trained a nucleus of American rabbis at the Hebrew Union College (founded in 1875) that he was able to organize a conference that could endure. As a matter of fact, he originally thought of even this Conference as being only sectional. In his address to the CCAR in 1894 he explained its name "Central Conference" by pointing out that there already existed two similar organizations, one in the South and one in the East; the new Conference was called "Central" as a geographical distinction. "It was supposed," he said, "that members would come, aside from alumni and faculty of the Hebrew Union College, from the Central States ... The supposition proved incorrect, for the Conference ... is truly national."

Although Wise had attempted in his earlier years to bring together Orthodox and Reform rabbis, by the time the CCAR was organized he had come to the conclusion that only an association of homogeneous elements would succeed. In his address to the third annual convention in 1892 he said that from the very start the Conference excluded the so-called conservatives; and he made the same point in his address the following year when he declared that only representatives of the progressive school were accepted into membership.

The Conference was formally organized in Detroit, Michigan, in 1889, by some 30 rabbis who were attending the Biennial Assembly of the Union of American Hebrew Congregations in that city. Isaac Mayer Wise was elected its first president, an office that he held until his death in 1900.

The constitution, which was adopted at the 1890 convention in Cleveland, declared that "all matters pertaining to Judaism, its literature and its welfare are legitimate business for the Conference." In addition to the usual organizational machinery, it provided for the publication of a *Yearbook* and the establishment of a relief fund. Samuel Adler, the only surviving member in the United States (other than Wise) of the rabbinical conferences held in Germany after 1840, was elected honorary president of the Conference. The proceedings of all the modern rabbinical conferences, beginning with that which was held in Braunschweig in 1844, were accepted as the "basis" for the ideology of the Conference, "in an endeavor to maintain, in unbroken historic succession, the formulated expression of Jewish thought and life of each era." Although all of the declarations of past Reform conferences were printed in the *Yearbook* (including the responses of the Napoleonic Sanhedrin of 1807!), none was specifically endorsed as the "platform" of the new Conference.

In his address to the 1890 convention of the Conference, Wise proclaimed the right of American rabbis as a group to distinguish between living and dead religious forms and customs. He insisted that it was the duty and right of the Conference to defend Judaism from stagnation, and to support the rabbis as individuals against recrimination. At the same time he asserted the need for consultation and mutual agreement as a hedge against total anarchy. "All reforms," he said,

> ought to go into practice on the authority of the Conference, not only to protect the individual rabbi, but to protect Judaism against presumptuous innovations and the precipitations of rash and inconsiderate men. The Conference is the lawful authority in all matters of form.

The Conference, however, has never assumed formal legislative authority. Wise, himself, in his 1898 presidential address, declared that the Conference never commanded but only advised. Since his time the CCAR has consistently held to this view in regard to its decisions on religious matters and social issues. In 1949, when the Executive Board was asked to note that some CCAR members were ignoring positions recommended in the *Rabbi's Manual*, the Executive Board responded that the Conference had never attempted to compel its members to abide by its recommendations and pronouncements, but regarded itself rather as a guide.

At first some of the eastern rabbis remained aloof from the Conference; the antagonism between Reform rabbis in the East and the Midwest was not sectional only, but more directly related to theology — the Easterners being inclined to be more radical. But in 1892 Joseph Silverman of Temple Emanu-El invited the Conference to meet in New York City. According to Wise, the invitation was readily accepted; he hoped this would change the habit of some Easterners of calling anything outside New York "Western" and of referring to the Central Conference as the "Western Conference." The meeting in New York dissolved some of the hostility, and the Conference gained several new members in New York and vicinity, among them Kohler, Benjamin, and Leucht. But Gottheil did not attend, leaving the city a few hours before the meetings began with no attempt to explain his departure.

If the Conference had no authority to legislate, it nevertheless brought order into a hitherto chaotic Reform movement. Its first effort in this direction was the creation of a new prayerbook. In his address to the 1890 convention of the Conference, Isaac M. Wise pleaded for the publication of a uniform form of worship, which could only be accomplished by the Conference. His appeal was successful, and a liturgical committee was immediately appointed. By 1892, Volume I of the *Union Prayer Book* was published and accepted as the authorized ritual of the CCAR; and, in 1894 Volume II, for the High Holidays, appeared. Within a year of its publication the *Union Prayer Book* was adopted by 55 congregations; by the turn of the century it was in use in some 125 congregations. Although some congregations continued well into the 1920s to use prayerbooks that had been compiled by their individual rabbis, the *Union Prayer Book* became the accepted ritual of the Reform movement as a whole. This liturgy underwent two revisions, of Volume I in 1940 and of Volume II in 1945. This *Prayer Book* was one of the most important factors in unifying the Reform movement in the United States. Prior to the publication of the *Union Prayer Book*, the wide variety of prayerbooks in use created a chaotic situation that tended to emphasize the distinctiveness and separateness of each congregation. The *Union Prayer Book* brought cohesiveness to the Reform movement, and brought its rabbis and congregants closer together.

The *Union Prayer Book* was followed by the *Union Hymnal*, which first appeared in 1897 and was subsequently revised in 1914 and again in 1932. The *Union Songster*, a volume of songs, hymns, and services for Jewish youth, was published in 1960.

The *Haggadah* was first appended to the *Union Prayer Book*, but the Conference decided to eliminate it from future printings and to publish it in separate form. Several years passed before an acceptable version was finally adopted in 1908, which was published in revised form in 1923.

The first *Minister's Handbook* appeared in 1917, succeeded by the *Rabbi's Manual* in 1928, a revised edition of which appeared in 1961. *Judaism*, a manual for proselytes, was published in 1928 and, in revised form in 1946. *Blessing and Praise*, a volume of meditations and prayers for private devotion, was published in 1923 but was replaced by the *Union Home Prayer Book* in 1951. The latter volume, which contains a variety of prayers for family worship and for personal devotion, includes some of the material previously published in *Blessing and Praise*.

In the early years the sale of the *Union Prayer Book* was the responsibility of one of the members of the CCAR, who received a commission for his efforts. Later the Bloch Publishing Company became the sole agent for Conference publications, an arrangement that continued to about 1925. Since that time the Conference has itself supervised the distribution of its publications. The income realized from the sale of its publications has been the chief support for Conference expenditures.

For many years the Conference entertained the idea of publishing a journal. In 1908, when the original British *Jewish Quarterly Review* suspended publication, the Conference deliberated the desirability of issuing its own periodical, but this project was abandoned when Dropsie College announced that it planned to publish a new series of the *Jewish Quarterly Review*. In 1920 proposals to publish a homiletical journal as well as a projected journal of Jewish lore and philosophy were discussed, but although the Conference did not undertake publication of either, the *Hebrew Union College Annual* stemmed from a similar proposal made to the Hebrew Union College Board of Governors regarding the *Journal of Jewish Lore and Philosophy*. In 1920 a resolution to establish a journal of Jewish religion and ethics was considered, and in 1948 a proposal to publish a journal of homiletics was advanced. Finally, in 1953, the *CCAR Journal,* a quarterly periodical, was established. It has become a genuine forum for the expression of CCAR members' ideas on a variety of themes, including the homiletical, academic, theological, professional, and social fields. It has already published more issues than any other rabbinical periodical.

Among other Conference publications were an annual sermon pamphlet (following the precedent established in 1896 when it published a volume of sermons) and a series of tracts. Both later became a cooperative venture with the Union of American Hebrew Congregations, the tracts being published under the title,

"Popular Studies." The Conference has also published in pamphlet form the *Weekday Afternoon and Evening Services for the Synagogue and House of Mourning*, a service for Confirmation-Shavuos, and an experimental commentary to the first Friday evening service of the *Union Prayer Book*.

In 1961 the Conference published the *Israel Bettan Memorial Volume* in tribute to its president who had died in office. Annually, of course, the CCAR publishes a *Yearbook* which includes a digest of the Conference meeting proceedings, reports of its committees and commissions, papers and addresses, and directories. As the oldest annual publication in American Jewish life, it is an inexhaustible source of research data about the history of the American Jewish community as well as of the Reform movement.

A matter of historical interest in the area of publications was the cooperation of the Conference with the Jewish Publication Society of America in the creation of its English translation of the Bible.

Throughout its history the Conference has cooperated in many areas and in a variety of ways with other organizations, both general and Jewish. A perennial concern of the Conference has been that of bringing some order into the competing, conflicting, and duplicating activities of national Jewish organizations.

The Conference has always enjoyed close relations with the Union of American Hebrew Congregations. A number of joint commissions have functioned creatively throughout the years. Although there have been issues of conflict and differences of emphasis between the Union and Conference, these have become the object of violent opposition very rarely. The president of the UAHC is an *ex-officio* member of the Executive Board of the Conference, and the Conference elects several representatives to the Board of Trustees of the Union.

Beginning in 1914 the Conference appointed representatives to the Advisory Board of the Board of Governors — and later to the Board of Governors itself — of the Hebrew Union College. This arrangement came to an end when in 1946 the president of the College requested the CCAR to discontinue naming representatives to the Board of Governors when the terms of those then serving expired; and this prerogative was turned over to the Hebrew Union College Alumni Association. By this time a considerable number of members of the Conference were graduates of the Jewish Institute of Religion, and the Conference had no official representation on the board of the JIR. With the merger of the HUC and the JIR, which the Conference hailed with satisfaction, this reason no longer existed, and not long after the merger the Conference entered upon discussions with the HUC-JIR to reinstitute Conference representation on the board of the merged seminary.

The lack of such representation has been a source of concern to the Conference, which has felt that a closer relationship would be of mutual benefit to the College-Institute and the CCAR. Discussions with the College-Institute authorities were revived in the early 1960s, and although legal and technical difficulties were cited as a problem, it was hoped that a way might be found to reestablish the kind of official relationship that existed previously with the HUC. The members of the Conference and the Conference as a body have felt a loyalty to the College-Institute and have rejoiced in its expanded program. The president of the HUC-JIR is, by provision of the CCAR bylaws, an *ex-officio* member of the CCAR Executive Board.

It was the initiative of the CCAR that led to the founding of the Synagogue Council of America. Abram Simon, in his presidential message, broached the subject and a call was extended to Conservative and Orthodox groups to form a national body of rabbinical and congregational organizations, which resulted in the establishment in 1926 of the Synagogue Council of America. The Conference ever since has played an active role in this organization.

It was in the same year that the World Union for Progressive Judaism was founded, at the call of Lily H. Montague. Members of the Conference attended the meeting held in London that year and at a special convention of the Conference held the following January, the Conference officially became a constituent organization.

A number of ideological controversies have occupied the attention of the Conference in the course of its history. In the early years there was the question of a synod. The matter of authority has been before the Conference in several forms. For a long time the question of formulating a theology of Reform Judaism agitated the Conference. The advisability of adopting a statement of principles was debated and finally resolved when the Conference adopted the "Guiding Principles of Reform Judaism" at the convention in Columbus, Ohio, in 1937. Another controversial issue was the question of Zionism.

Among the ideological controversies was the question of approval of major Sunday morning services. Many congregations had introduced such services; the issue was whether sanctioning such services would lead to the weakening of the Sabbath and perhaps even to the eventual substitution of Sunday for the Saturday Sabbath. In 1903 the Conference adopted a motion declaring itself in favor of maintaining the historical Sabbath. The following year, while recognizing the historical Sabbath as a bond of unity with Israel the world over, the Conference resolved that since economic and industrial conditions made it impossible for large numbers to attend services on the seventh day, the spirit of Judaism was not opposed to the conduct of worship on Sunday or any other weekday wherever the necessity was felt. This required the provision of an adequate service for those congregations that worshiped on Sunday; and in 1906 it was agreed that six weekday services be printed for a year's provisional use. Some years later it was suggested that the weekday services be designated Sunday Services but this proposal was defeated; as late as 1931 the Liturgy Committee was instructed by the Executive Board to prepare sets of Sunday services with the assistance of members who conducted such services. In 1933 the Liturgy Committee, then engaged in the revision of the *Prayer Book*, reported that it would begin its work with the weekday services since Sunday services had increased.

Soon after that time, however, the popularity of Sunday services began to wane, and virtually every congregation that had previously conducted a Sunday morning service moved its major service to Friday night. As of this writing, indeed, probably more congregations conduct daily services than ever conducted major services on Sunday morning.

The question of mixed marriage has from time to time erupted in the Conference. After a long discussion in 1909 a resolution was adopted declaring that "mixed marriages are contrary to the tradition of the Jewish religion and should therefore be discouraged by the American rabbinate." The issue was the subject of a major debate in 1947, but after long discussion, the 1909 resolution was reaffirmed. In the late 1950s and early 1960s it was felt that the position of the Conference should be re-examined; in 1962 a Special Committee on Mixed Marriage made two recommendations in its report. One was for a permanent committee to concern itself with mixed marriage and the range of problems related to it. The other was a new official statement relaxing somewhat the traditional Conference stand, which most members had interpreted to mean that a rabbi should refuse to officiate at mixed marriages. The first recommendation, for a committee to study the problems, was adopted. The second was tabled, leaving the original resolution of 1909 as the official position of the Conference. Yet discussions and surveys continued; public controversy over the meaning and extent of the problem of intermarriage justified the Conference's decision to establish a permanent committee to deal with the problem.

The supreme authority of the Conference is its annual convention. It is here that the position of the Conference is adopted on issues that come before it. The Executive Board administers the business of the Conference between conventions, but its actions are subject to Conference approval. A large part of the work of the Conference is entrusted to its committees. In the early years there were few committees, the most important being Ritual, Hymnal, Publication, Ethics, Superannuated Ministers' Fund, Sabbath Question, and a few others. Gradually the number of committees increased, with standing committees being established in the fields of Church and State, Arbitration (later called Mediation and Ethics), History, Religious Education, Responsa, Social Justice (combined some years ago with the Committee on Peace and re-named Justice and Peace), Liturgy, Chaplaincy, Synagogue Music, and many others. By 1964 there were 29 standing committees, three special interest groups, several special committees, and six joint commissions with the Union of American Hebrew Congregations.

As far back as 1907 proposals were made to consider the advisability of setting up a pension plan for rabbis. During the succeeding decades a number of plans were presented, but none really seemed to offer promise of meeting the problem. Finally, in 1944, a pension plan was established in cooperation with the Union of American Hebrew Congregations. The plan is operated by the Rabbinical Pension Board which is comprised of an equal number of representatives of the Conference and of the Union.

The question of placement has been of concern to the Conference almost from the beginning. As early as 1900 the president objected to the trial sermon. For some years, beginning in 1907, the question of a Pulpit Bureau was considered. Throughout the years constant dissatisfaction was expressed over the manner in which pulpits were filled. Finally, in 1950, the Conference adopted a plan proposed by a Joint Placement Commission of the Conference and the Union which would have been obligatory on both rabbis and congregations. The plan, however, was defeated at the Union Biennial that year. A Provisional Rabbinical Placement Committee composed of one representative each of the Conference, Union, and HUC-JIR was set up and functioned with some degree of success. At the convention in 1961 a plan that is mandatory for rabbis and that provides for a placement director on the staff of the Conference was adopted, and the Union and College-Institute were invited to participate in the establishment of a Rabbinical Placement Commission under the terms of this plan. The Union's Biennial Assembly and the Board of Governors of the HUC-JIR both gave approval to the plan; the Commission was appointed; and Rabbi Malcolm H. Stern was named its first full-time director in 1964.

From time to time, in its earlier years, the Conference expressed its disapproval of regional organizations. In 1904 the president questioned the usefulness of the Southern Rabbinical Conference. In 1913, when an Eastern Council of Reform Rabbis was formed, the Conference voiced its fear that sectional conferences would make for division, and officially discouraged the formation of Reform rabbinical associations other than those in metropolitan areas. When the Western Association of Reform Rabbis was organized in 1946, the Conference expressed its apprehension, and the Executive Board notified the newly-formed Association that it should limit itself to purely regional matters.

In time, however, with the growth of Conference membership, it was recognized that regional organizations could serve a legitimate function. A number of city-wide bodies had already been formed, and there were also some organizations of a regional character. There were, indeed, other groups of rabbis meeting informally. The need for formal regional organization and direction was becoming increasingly evident. In 1955 the Conference officially expressed formal approval of regional groups and urged a closer relationship between them and the Conference, with safeguards so that there would be no divided voices representing the Reform rabbinate. By 1964 there were 10 groups operating as regional organizations of the Conference.

The Conference has encouraged scholarship, providing modest but essential subventions to scholars and organizations doing scholarly work. In 1929 and for several years thereafter, the Conference received substantial grants for this purpose from the Littauer Fund. The Conference annually allocates a sum from its income for academic subventions.

When in the 1920s, as an outcome of World War I, the seminaries of Central Europe were in severe financial distress, the Conference established a fund to provide them with financial assistance. During the Hitler period, the Conference gave financial aid to refugee rabbis and freely admitted many from Germany to its ranks, doing its utmost to help them secure pulpits.

For a number of years after World War II, the Conference conducted institutes through its various committees. Several of these were held under the auspices of the Committee on Justice and Peace. There were also Institutes on Psychiatry and Religion; on Theology; and on Marriage, Family and the Home. Valuable reports came out of some of these institutes. In some cases embarrassment to the Conference was caused when press reports gave the impression that the decisions of these institutes were those of the Conference, whereas in actual fact only a small proportion of the Conference membership participated. Although these institutes were called national and all CCAR members were invited to them, they usually attracted only rabbis from the vicinity in which they were held. They were discontinued with the development of regional organizations, for which the Conference now provides regional seminars.

Another important activity of the Conference, that of providing chaplains for the Armed Forces of the United States, was established during World War II.

The Conference has grown from a very small group to almost 900 members in 1964. In its early years the core of the Conference was made up of the graduates and faculty of the Hebrew Union College. As time went on, with more and more classes graduating from the HUC, and older, European-trained rabbis passing away, these graduates came to make up almost all of the Conference membership. With the graduation of the first class of the Jewish Institute of Religion, however, a new group began to join the Conference, and in succeeding years the diversity of Conference membership increased. In the 1930s the Conference welcomed émigré colleagues from Germany. The complexion of the Conference changed from a homogeneous group of alumni of the same theological seminary to a more varied membership. This situation created certain tensions. The vested interests of the HUC alumni were being challenged. The warmth and closeness of earlier years no longer existed. With the merger of the two rabbinical schools into the HUC-JIR, the tensions, of course, have diminished; one hardly recognizes today who is a graduate of the one school and who of the other. These divisions and rivalries have ceased to exist. But if the Conference is unified in this respect, its very growth has made for diversity. It is no longer the small, intimate group it was. If it has gained in strength, its very size presents problems that will not easily be solved.

For most of its existence the Conference was run without any headquarters. If there was a semblance of a central office, it was that of the Administrative Secretary, Rabbi Isaac E. Marcuson, who served as secretary for over 30 years and operated most of the business of the Conference from his own temple office. Finally, with the death of Rabbi Marcuson in 1952, and with the recognition by the membership that the activities and needs of the Conference required full-time service, the Conference decided to appoint an Executive Vice President and to establish headquarters in New York City (1954).

In earlier days, before other national rabbinical organizations took an interest in larger social issues, the voice of the Conference was the only one representing the Jewish religious point of view. Today, while the Conference still makes its own pronouncements, its voice is but one among many. Its actions are not always as direct as they formerly were but are frequently taken through the coordinating bodies with which it is affiliated. There is a gain in that the purposes for which the Conference worked so long practically single-handedly are now furthered through Jewish organizations representative of the wider Jewish community. The Conference loses, however, a sense of the direct participation we had in former days.

The size of the Conference, with its membership scattered throughout the country, poses a problem in committee organization. In the early years committees were small enough to operate effectively. As the Conference grew in numbers, however, committees became so large that (with the exception of a few such as the Liturgy Committee which was deliberately kept small since it had to meet if it was to produce the material required of it) they were unable to hold meetings, and much of the work was done through correspondence. Sometimes, and this tended to become the rule, the chair did the work without consulting the members of his/her committee. This was remedied to some extent by the appointment of a steering group of each committee which was given a budget for traveling expenses. By 1964 it was still unclear whether this would solve the problem or whether it would be necessary to limit drastically the size of committees, with a large proportion of CCAR members not serving on any committee.

The size of the Conference and its traditions often make for slowness in getting things done. By tradition, the text of any devotional material published by the Conference must have the approval of the Conference as a whole. It is first considered line by line by the responsible committee, in itself a long and laborious process; it frequently takes years before a text is ever submitted to the Conference itself. Then it must receive final approval from the Conference at a convention, which frequently returns it to the relevant committee with suggestions for further revision, resulting, of course, in further delay. When a liturgical composition is finally published the Conference does not attribute authorship to any individual or group of individuals. Not even the names of the members of the committee appear in the published work. It is regarded as the product of the entire Conference.

The Conference position on issues of the day is not easily determined. On some public issues the Conference has already adopted a position that can be applied to specific circumstances; the officers are therefore empowered to speak for the Conference even though it is not in session. But when new issues arise, only the members assembled in convention can resolve a new question or adopt a new policy.

The members of the Conference are jealous of their prerogatives. They are rarely willing to delegate authority. They want to participate in decisions of the Conference. When the Conference was smaller and life moved more slowly, this did not constitute a problem. This policy provided for democratic discussion of all matters. With a large membership and with events moving rapidly, some decisions have to be made more quickly than is possible under the cumbersome machinery that reserves final authority to a single, annual convention. One of the Conference's major dilemmas by 1964 was whether more authority should be delegated or whether the more cautious process of arriving at a course of action was still the preferable procedure. Every organization, as it grows larger, becomes to some extent unwieldy. It has to re-evaluate old traditions and practices and to determine how to adjust to the problems presented by the enlarged nature of its organization and by the changing times.

Liberal though it may be in its views, the Conference is basically very conservative in changing its own procedures. Perhaps it is just because its members are intensely individualistic, prizing their personal freedom as religious leaders in their own communities, that they want the Conference as a corporate body to represent a corporate consensus rather than the views of those colleagues who happen to be officers at a given time. If this makes for slower action, that may be the price that the Conference is willing to pay to guard against any kind of bureaucracy or ecclesiasticism. How far procedures should be modified is a matter of continuing concern.

The Conference completed its first 75 years with a large measure of achievement. Its underlying purposes, as its activities throughout these years indicate, have been to serve its members, to advance the cause of Judaism, and to express the position of the Reform Jewish rabbinate on the social and moral issues of the day.

Part II: 1964-1989

ELLIOT L. STEVENS

This section presents a summary of developments within the CCAR during the quarter-century since the Conference celebrated its 75th anniversary in 1964. It addresses the evolving programs and concerns of the CCAR as it neared its centennial, as well as structural changes within the Conference itself.

Conference Structure

We start with a look at changes in the demographic make-up of the CCAR over the past 25 years.

When Sidney L. Regner cast his eye back on Conference history in *Retrospect and Prospect* (1964), the CCAR counted 912 members. In that same year, the new Director of Placement, Malcolm H. Stern, submitted his first report to the *Yearbook*, including a demographic breakdown of Conference membership. Comparing his report with the 1990 report filed by his successor, A. Stanley Dreyfus, we find that while Conference membership increased 69 percent, to 1544 (not including the Class of 1990), those serving as full-time rabbis in congregations increased only 49 percent, with a relatively small but growing minority serving outside the Reform rabbinate. At the same time, those reporting "secular" occupations increased by 144 percent, overseas rabbis by 236 percent, and retirees by 342 percent. Clearly, occupational categories among members of the CCAR have broadened to an unprecedented degree, leading to new challenges regarding the Conference's responsiveness to the concerns of its changing population. By the mid-1980s, approximately one-half of all CCAR members were *not* serving in full-time congregational positions. The changing demography of the CCAR also included the rising numbers of women rabbis since the ordination of Sally J. Priesand in 1972. By the CCAR centennial, roughly 10 percent of Conference membership was female, with a likelihood that the near-equivalency of numbers of men and women entering the College-Institute would augment that proportion in years to come.

Responding to the trend toward diversification, the Executive Board in 1973 created a standing Committee on the Varieties of Rabbinic Experience, mandating the committee to monitor statistics, provide convention workshops, and work with the different constituencies, the better to understand and promote each one's relationship with the CCAR. The aim of utilizing the skills of these groups of rabbis — Hillel directors, agency executives, chaplains both military and institutional, those serving in helping professions or "secular" occupations — led in turn to the creation of Specialist Councils in 1987, based on proposals from then-President Eugene J. Lipman. As a result, more non-congregational rabbis have been placed on committees, on the Executive Board, and on convention programs.

The expanding membership of the Conference saw a parallel increase in the structures and complexity of the organization. Regional and sub-regional groupings proliferated as members sought new opportunities for local collegiality and participation. Before 1960, the several regional groups — most notably the Western Association of Reform Rabbis (now PARR) formed decades earlier — had only tenuous ties with the national body. In that year, a Committee on Regional Organization provided the first model regional constitution and, more important, new support for the integration of regional structures into the life of the Conference. By 1965, a Committee on Conference Structure won Executive Board support for the creation of new regions under a national structural umbrella, including national administration of scholars' programs at *kallot* and visitations by national staff. Regional presidents for the first time were invited, at their own expense, to attend pre- and post-convention meetings of the Executive Board. In 1971, regional representation on the board was formalized, by amendment to the constitution, to provide for full membership of regional delegates on the board. At the centennial, 12 regions were represented on the board, along with the officers and eight members elected "at large."

The expanding interests of Conference members also led to the restructuring of the committee system. Before 1965, most standing committees had open memberships, but these were reduced by Executive Board action that year to a statutory limit of seven in the hope that smaller committees would be able to meet more often and function more effectively. Recognizing, however, that the reductions would prevent many CCAR members from perhaps ever sitting on a committee, the Conference in 1973 approved new bylaws providing for a system of "open committees," whereby "corresponding members" would be listed on the roster without limit, and these could participate fully in committee meetings, although without reimbursement. Committees were instructed in the same bylaw to hold open meetings at conventions in order to broaden participation in their work.

At the centennial, the committee roster listed 27 standing committees; 26 joint commissions, task forces, and other representations; and 16 *ad hoc* committees, in the aggregate covering almost every identifiable rabbinic concern.

Of all the new sub-groups within the CCAR to emerge during this period, perhaps none has had as striking a success as NAORRR, the National Association of Retired Reform Rabbis. The proposal for a special grouping of retired or near-retired rabbis was presented by Paul Gorin in 1982 to the Executive Board, which endorsed the project with enthusiasm. NAORRR held its first conference in 1984 in Orlando. It now attracts to its annual gatherings more than 100, including rabbinic widows. The meetings are unusually warm and congenial, aside from their programs on scholarly topics, placement opportunities, the exploration of retirement benefits, and like matters.

Matching the rise in Conference structures, the CCAR office itself expanded, since a first national office was authorized in 1953 and opened in two rooms in the New York school of HUC-JIR in 1954. The selection of Malcolm H. Stern as the first Director of Placement in 1964 led to a move to larger quarters at 790 Madison Avenue, with some 1,000 square feet. A third executive rabbi, Elliot L. Stevens, joined the staff as Administrative Secretary and Director of Publications in 1975. The addition of new secretarial staff required another move, to 21 East 40th Street, in 1981, and in 1987 to 192 Lexington Avenue.

At the centennial, the CCAR staff numbered three executive rabbis and seven supporting staff persons in quarters of nearly 4,700 square feet. The office had been rounded out in 1988 with the addition of the Rabbinical Pension Board as a tenant of the CCAR.

The executive staff of the CCAR has been remarkably stable over the years. In 1971, Joseph B. Glaser was elected successor to Sidney L. Regner as Executive Vice President, and in 1982 he received a life contract. Elliot L. Stevens was granted tenure in 1984. In the Placement Office, A. Stanley Dreyfus succeeded Malcolm H. Stern in 1979. His successor, Arnold I. Sher, was elected at the centennial convention to assume the position of Director of Placement in 1990.

Programs and Services

While this summary cannot describe in any significant detail the many concerns addressed by the Conference over the years, primarily through its committees, a review of several programs will indicate the extent to which the members of the CCAR have tried to respond to the changing needs of the (primarily) North American Reform rabbinate.

One frustration often expressed by individual members of the Conference is their lack of time or opportunity to engage in serious study of rabbinic texts or to keep up with developments in Judaic scholarship. As the role of the rabbi has evolved further away from that of decisor of Jewish law into today's multifaceted rabbinate, many rabbis have felt it necessary to devote themselves more to the acquisition of practical skills while neglecting Jewish source materials and academic disciplines. The CCAR itself has felt the need for programs of continuing rabbinic education when, for example, the Conference's Committee on Responsa has openings that must be filled only by rabbis comfortable with the sources.

Over the last quarter-century, the CCAR has sought to encourage rabbinic study, to promote continuing studies through the College-Institute and the Alumni Association, and to create its own programs. In 1964, with the opening of the Jerusalem School of HUC-JIR, the CCAR adopted a resolution calling for all rabbinic students to engage in a year of study at that campus to sharpen their Hebraic and rabbinic skills; the matter was referred to the College-Institute which six years later undertook such a program for all entering students.

Not all recommendations were as successfully implemented. In 1972, the Executive Board established a new Committee on Continuing Rabbinic Education that was mandated to cooperate with HUC-JIR. In 1978, with a program not yet in evidence, the committee proposed a program of "certification" for rabbis completing certain levels of study, to be based on the model of "Continuing Education Units" (CEUs) tracked by some other associations. The proposal was referred by the board for discussions with HUC-JIR and the Alumni Association. Again in 1984, the CCAR's Committee on Professional Growth called in its annual report for a CEU program to be implemented together with the College-Institute and Alumni Association. In 1990 the CCAR Executive Board gave its approval to a similar proposal by a reconstituted Committee on Continuing Education.

The creation in 1989 of a new body designated a Task Force on Continuing Education, mandated to bring together representatives of the CCAR, HUC-JIR, and other rabbis in academia and to work with the Standing Committee on Continuing Education, assured the creation of new courses alongside the already substantial alumni offerings of the College-Institute. The new task force planned to organize academic convocations and to establish an academy for rabbinic studies to augment the program of studies at conventions and regional *kallot*. The founding of a Sabbatical Academy in Jerusalem in 1988 and the organization into a "library," starting in 1975, of more than a thousand conference educational tapes rounded out the continuing education program.

Parallel to long-standing calls for programs of continuing education, the enlargement and professionalization of the CCAR led to increasing concerns for the rabbi's personal growth and the quality of the inner life of the rabbi. A Committee on Professional Rabbinic Growth, created in 1980, concluded at its first meeting (1981) that an exploration of personal rabbinic spirituality and faith was urgently needed. Members of the committee felt that many rabbis are so occupied by their day-to-day responsibilities that religious thinking, exploration, and practice become next to impossible. Accordingly, the committee sponsored a Conference on Rabbinic Faith and Spirituality in Mohonk, New York, in November 1981, reaching its registration limit of 50 rabbis almost as soon as the conference was announced. A second nationally-sponsored event was held near Chicago in 1984, after which most regions of the CCAR instituted their own spirituality conferences. These conferences provided a welcome opportunity for rabbis to share their spiritual doubts and quests in an empathetic environment.

Similar in its dynamic, although with a different focus, was the career review program, the need for which was first hinted by President Roland B. Gittelsohn and Vice President David Polish in their joint convention address of 1971 when they called for a regionalized program of rabbis' rabbis, to counsel colleagues in need. Accordingly, an *ad hoc* committee, called at the time Mid-Career Review, was created in 1974. In 1976 it sponsored a first review, using part of a $25,000 grant from the Charles E. Merrill Trust. That and subsequent reviews brought together a dozen or so rabbis and a rabbi-psychologist, together with one or two senior rabbinic "mentors," in an isolated retreat setting without direct CCAR staff involvement. There, with complete confidentiality, rabbis who had experienced personal uncertainty, or angst, or *wanderlust* could reinvigorate or redirect their rabbinic careers. Both the spirituality conferences and the career review programs have won the acclaim of our membership.

Yet another closely-related program was created by the Executive Board in 1982, to provide career counseling to rabbis who might not have need of a full-scale career review, but might feel themselves in need of counseling in a particular area of rabbinic functioning. In this program, a coordinator refers colleagues to area specialists for assistance.

Emergency counseling for rabbis and their families was made available in 1977 with the introduction by the Family Life Committee of a Rabbinic Family Hot Line. Calls were taken by a rabbi with professional credentials in family therapy. More than 100 confidential calls were made on the hot line in its first dozen years of service.

Just as the regional groups took on a greater role within the CCAR during the 1960s and 1970s, so demographic constituencies developed structures of their own, reflecting members' needs for greater intimacy and interrelation than was possible on a national level. NAORRR, the organization of retirees, has been mentioned. In 1979, a Small Cities Committee was formed to serve rabbis in smaller or more isolated communities. Within a year, some 250 rabbis were on a master list and receiving a quarterly newsletter reflecting concerns of rabbis in small congregations. Rabbinic spouses formed a Spouse Support Group in 1984, regionalizing the following year and also publishing a newsletter. Both the Small Cities Committee and the Spouse Support Group offer annual programs at CCAR conventions; the latter sponsors programs at many annual regional meetings as well.

The field of rabbinic finances has not been neglected. Already in 1965 a proposal was made to the Executive Board for a survey of rabbinic compensation, to be sponsored jointly with the Department of Synagogue Administration of the UAHC. The motion failed but a special committee was appointed four years later to consider the financial needs of Conference members. Suggestions for a survey continued, and after several regions undertook their own during the 1970s, a national survey was finally undertaken during the 1980-81 year; since then, the full-time congregational rabbinate has been surveyed annually with a better-than-98-percent rate of response. Mark L. Winer has been in charge of this helpful project since its inception.

One sub-group of rabbis within the CCAR saw its role redefined and diminished over the last quarter-century. Required service in the military chaplaincy began during World War II, and successfully met the nation's need for Jewish military chaplains through the war in Vietnam; at the height of the war in Vietnam the number of Reform rabbis in uniform was greater than that of both Conservative and Orthodox rabbis combined. In the late 1960s the senior chaplains in the Army, Navy, and Air Force were all members of the CCAR, as was Aryeh Lev, the professional executive head of the Joint Chaplaincy Commission of the National Jewish Welfare Board.

Throughout this period rabbis professing their conscientious objection to military service could apply for exemptions. As protest against American involvement in Vietnam grew, individual rabbis asked for the institution of "selective" conscientious objection in order to express their reluctance to serve in what an increasing number felt to be an unjust war. Such a provision was adopted by the CCAR at its 1968 convention. At the same convention, an extended debate on the chaplaincy itself, particularly concerning proposals for alternate forms of service in place of mandatory service in the military, led to referral of the issues to a special committee that was asked to report to the 1969 convention.

That year brought another lengthy and, at times, emotional debate on a particular motion: "...to abolish the chaplaincy draft for a period of two years, after which it is to be reviewed to determine whether we are meeting the needs of the Jewish men in the Armed Forces." During the debate a series of motions was made providing for a civilian alternative to the chaplaincy or for a quota system of voluntary service. One proposal suggested that each new class of ordinees would have its own quota but that service would, nonetheless, somehow be voluntary. All such motions were defeated, and the two-year abolition of the chaplaincy draft was adopted and later extended through 1973 at which time the decline in conscription ended further discussion of non-voluntary chaplaincy service. The CCAR's Committee on Chaplaincy's role became primarily one of recruitment until 1981 when its mandate was expanded to include within its purview prison and hospital chaplaincies. An extended report of the committee's activities in the period following the Vietnam war appears in the *Yearbook* of 1976 (p. 24).

CCAR Finances

The burgeoning activities of the CCAR in the 1970s and 1980s often outran the Conference's ability to finance them, providing a major financial challenge to the Conference and its leadership.

The story is related in part through the CCAR's budget. In 1964, actual income of the CCAR totaled $387,641, compared with expenditures of $277,829. Since segregation of funds used for relief and subventions was not accomplished until 1981, these numbers represent *all* funds of the Conference. In 1989, the centennial year, total income (including restricted funds for comparison purposes) was $1,747,171 against total expenses of $1,315,966. The apparent surplus occurred exclusively within the restricted portion of the Conference budget (due primarily to income from the Centennial Fund Drive; see below). When the restricted columns are removed from the financial statement of 1989, the CCAR actually finished the year with a deficit of $86,689.

Remarkably, the income categories of dues, publications, and investment returns accounted for the same proportions of Conference income at the end of this period as at the beginning, as indeed they have done since the turn of the century. Dues have provided about 15 percent of Conference income, publications about 70 percent, and investment returns the other 15 percent. Dues were $5 annually until 1952 when the first sliding scale of dues payments based on rabbinic salaries was inaugurated.

As programs and services proliferated, even the expanding budget was insufficient to meet these needs, and deficit financing, sometimes on a substantial level, became more common. In the years 1972, 1973, and 1974, deficits exceeded $100,000 *each year*, as congregations awaited the CCAR's introduction of a new prayerbook for the Reform movement. As a result, the Conference portfolio shrank from nearly $1 million to less than one-fifth of that amount. In 1975, the publication of *Gates of Prayer* assured the CCAR of recuperative surpluses that for the ensuing five years averaged more than $200,000 annually. The success of the prayerbook and its High Holiday companion, *Gates of Repentance*, published in 1978, made possible many of the programs mentioned in the previous section.

The financial crisis and its resolution call for fuller explanation. Throughout the 1960s, demands were voiced for a new *Union Prayer Book*, which, in its several editions since the 1890s, had probably done more to unify the Reform movement than any other single factor. As proposals and ideas were shared through the *CCAR Journal*, at conventions, and elsewhere, a special symposium was called in November 1966, to consider issues of liturgy and worship, and in particular to provide a critical evaluation of the *Union Prayer Book*. The following year, in 1967, Sidney L. Regner, in his Executive Vice President's report to the convention, called for the development of a new prayerbook and the project was undertaken by the Committee on Liturgy.

As experimental services began to circulate, sales of the *Union Prayer Book* declined. They dropped dramatically after President Roland B. Gittelsohn announced in his 1971 presidential address that a new prayerbook was on the way. This prayerbook, as endorsed in December 1970 by the Executive Board, was to contain a broad selection of prayers culled from the experimental liturgies, together with "the best of" the *Union Prayer Book*. A March 1971 draft was approved by the board, but it quickly became apparent that the new volume could not satisfy the movement's needs, nor compete with an attractive prayerbook, *Service of the Heart*, which had just been published by the Union of Liberal and Progressive Synagogues in London. With the concurrence of the officers, Joseph B. Glaser, in one of his first acts as Executive Vice President, negotiated an agreement with the ULPS which allowed the CCAR to base its prayerbook (including, later, *Gates of Repentance*) on the British volumes in return for their agreement to cease marketing their works in North America. The Committee on Liturgy turned to Chaim Stern, who had co-edited the ULPS work and its companion *Gate of Repentance*, to draw on those works for approximately 30 percent of an American prayerbook. The agreement also called for royalty payments to be made by the CCAR to the ULPS, through a 15-year agreement (after which a "substantial revision" of the CCAR prayerbooks would bring an end to the CCAR's obligations.) This saved the CCAR from near bankruptcy. By its December 1971 meeting the board ratified the new arrangements and proceeded toward publication, which took place in 1975.

Although CCAR finances were much improved from then on, the Finance Committee, merged in 1971 with the Investments Committee, began to consider the establishment of an endowment fund to provide for long-term financial stability.

The Executive Board authorized an exploration of such a project in 1980, in order to increase its funds for the relief for retirees, widows, and others in need. After study by the Finance Committee, in 1983, the Executive Board adopted its plan for a $1 million Relief Endowment to be raised primarily from the membership. Relief had been one of the central concerns of the CCAR since its inception, indeed had been written into its charter when incorporation came in 1911. (Annual grants in 1990 to rabbis and rabbis' widows were projected to top $100,000 for the first time.)

The larger needs of the CCAR were then considered by the Finance Committee. In 1983, as the relief campaign began, Joseph B. Glaser proposed a centennial fund drive, which the Executive Board endorsed. By 1982 the CCAR had again entered an era of deficit financing (with some exceptions) as sales from the new prayerbooks began to diminish while the administrative costs of the CCAR's programs and services continued to expand. The Centennial Endowment developed into a $5 million program, in order to secure the future of the CCAR and its service to the Reform community. The laity were invited to contribute in honor of a beloved rabbi. By the centennial, more than half the endowment fund goal had been pledged, and more than two-thirds of the amount sought for the relief fund.

Publications

The single most important program of the Conference from a strictly financial point of view remained publications. During our period of review, the CCAR not only continued to emphasize its publication of congregational prayerbooks, but also expanded into broader areas, providing volumes for home and family use, guides to Jewish practice, and works of scholarship. The publication in 1972 of a *Shabbat Manual* proved to be something of a revolution in Reform movement publishing, as for the first time a guide to religious practice published by one of the movement's three national bodies, used the word *"mitzvah"* in its guidance to individual families. The work had derived from a 1965 convention symposium on the Sabbath which led to the creation of a Committee on the Sabbath (later, the Committee on Reform Jewish Practices). Earlier convention consideration of whether to publish such a guide to Jewish practice (notably one in 1959), had not been successful in coming to a consensus, some rabbis arguing that the very concept would undermine the ideological integrity of Reform Judaism. The public, meanwhile, showed itself unconcerned with the issue, and in three weeks bought up the first printing of 20,000 copies; the *Shabbat Manual* remained a strong seller for years. The committee brought out guides to the life cycle (*Gates of Mitzvah*, 1979) and to the Jewish year (*Gates of the Seasons*, 1983) and at the centennial was working on a volume about ethical *mitzvot*.

Another best-selling volume was *A Passover Haggadah*, published in 1974. Ten years in the making, this was the first CCAR publication to use full-color art, contemporary liturgical language, and music in a single volume. The *Haggadah* incorporated numerous additional readings and meditations to supplement the primary text. By the centennial, more than 600,000 copies had been sold.

Not every new publication was as successful. In 1984 the Conference published a new volume for festival worship which carried the title *The Five Scrolls*. With new translations of the biblical Scrolls, new liturgies, introductions, and full-color art, the CCAR anticipated that the book would appeal to non-Reform congregations and readers. Congregational, deluxe, and limited editions were all prepared, as were art posters, all produced to very high and, therefore, very expensive artistic and book-making standards. Unfortunately, with the exception of its congregational audience, the CCAR misjudged the market and suffered a financial setback.

While this article cannot cover every publication of the CCAR Press — a name in use since 1977 — mention may be made of *Judaism and Ethics* (1970), deriving from a symposium sponsored by the *Journal*; *Reform Judaism: A Historical Perspective* (1971), an anthology of articles from the *Yearbook*; *Rabbinic Authority* (1982), with papers from the 1980 convention on that theme; *Gates of the House* (1977); *Gates of Understanding* (Vol. I, 1977, and Vol. II, 1984); *American Reform Responsa* (1983) and *Contemporary American Reform Responsa* (1987); *The Six Days of Destruction* (1988), published with the Paulist Press for Yom Ha-Shoah and other Holocaust-related observances; laminated prayer cards for home use (1987); a new *Rabbi's Manual* (1988); *Gates of Healing* (1988); and *Seder Tu Bishevat* (1990). The publication, *Haneirot Halalu: These Lights Are Holy* (1989), was the CCAR's first book for home use by families at Chanuka; and *Gates of Wonder* (1990) was the first of a projected series of prayerbooks for children. With these and smaller booklets on retirement, interreligious activities, working with college students, adoption, and others, the CCAR Press at its centennial realized approximately $1,250,000 in gross annual sales, with surpluses of several hundred thousand dollars annually to support its operational program. At the same time, the CCAR maintained its agreement with the UAHC not to publish pedagogical works, while retaining exclusive right within the movement to publish liturgical materials. At its centennial, the CCAR Press employed the services of a consultant to its publications program, who reported that, of that consultant's hundreds of religious, associational, or corporate publishing clients, none came close to the surplus margins generated by the CCAR in its publishing.

Yet as the Conference neared its centennial, renewed talk of another prayerbook revision once again led to projections of deficits as sales of *Gates of Prayer* and *Gates of Repentance* fell from their earlier levels. As early as 1977, a convention paper on "The Restoration to Primacy of the Shabbat Morning Service," by Herbert Bronstein for the Commission on Worship, raised the desirability of creating new worship materials for Shabbat evening and morning services. In 1981, only six years after the appearance of *Gates of Prayer*, the Executive Board commissioned the Israeli poet T. Carmi to begin searching through the corpus of post-biblical Hebrew poetic materials for texts that might one day lend themselves to liturgical incorporation in a new CCAR prayerbook. Over the course of five years the "Carmi Project" identified hundreds of texts which were thematically organized and presented to the Liturgy Committee. Members of the committee submitted papers to the *Journal of Reform Judaism* (so-named in 1977) which provided critiques of *Gates of Prayer* on its 10th anniversary and reviewed a model for a new prayerbook introduced by Joseph Glaser in 1971. At the centennial (1989) the Executive Board approved a new congregational prayerbook as a long-term project, while also approving the publication of an interim Shabbat volume based on *Gates of Prayer* but providing gender-neutral language (a requirement for all CCAR publications since a board action in 1985).

Committees

In his annual Executive Vice President's report to the CCAR convention, Joseph B. Glaser often noted that the "real work" of the Conference takes place through its committees. As noted earlier, these number in the dozens, counting joint bodies with other agencies, especially the UAHC, and Conference representations outside the Reform movement. The annual reports of these committees reveal the extraordinary diversity of interest, expertise, and concerns of members of the CCAR.

Many committees have sponsored symposia or conferences as a means of exploring their missions or developing positions on the issues that made up their agenda. The following partial list is revealing of this diversity.

The 1968 symposium on Judaism and Ethics sponsored by the *CCAR Journal* has been mentioned. The *Journal* also sponsored a conference on "What Is Man?" in 1969. The Youth Committee held a conference on "Campus and Crisis" in 1969, and another in 1972 on "New Approaches to the Religious Experience." That committee also sponsored a conference in 1978 on "Cults and Conscience." In 1976, the Task Force on Jewish Identity held a conference on "Universalism and Particularism: The Language of Survival." The Israel Committee held a special convocation on Israel in 1983 with an explicit goal of producing an adoptable statement on Israel at that year's convention. Symposia were held on inflation (1980) and sexual values (1981), the latter sponsored by the Family Life Committee. That same committee also sponsored a series of conferences in 1985 and again in 1989, the latter focusing on pre-marital counseling. The Committee on Reform Jewish Practices held a conference on "The Rabbi's Personal Observance" in 1989, along the lines of the earlier spirituality conferences sponsored by the Committee on Rabbinic Growth. Many additional workshops were held by committees at the annual convention — sometimes as many as 18 in a year.

Committees of the Conference also engaged in study and prepared papers on Jewish or rabbinic issues for circulation or publication in the *Yearbook*. One such study, "The Psychodynamics of Jewish Identity and Survival," led to the creation of a special task force that functioned for five years culminating in the publication of a major paper in the 1979 *Yearbook*. Other papers issued included the study of Hebrew in congregations (1976, Commission on Religious Education); Jewish Family Planning (1977, Committee on Family Life); Jews in Arab Lands, and Cultic Proselytization (both produced in 1977 by the committees of the same names).

The Committee on Justice and Peace was especially prolific in its production of papers on world issues as seen from a liberal Jewish perspective. Issues addressed during the past 15 years include PACS, nuclear arms, "How to Deal with Your Enemies,"

"The Radical Right," abortion, and the environment. Such position papers provided more depth than was possible in a resolution, although several provided necessary background for subsequent resolutions. The papers were also seen as an adjunct to the Conference's responsa literature, which continued to address issues of Jewish practice by articulating a modern but tradition-respecting voice. The Committee on Justice and Peace also adopted several platform-like statements of principle — in 1918, 1920, 1928, 1960, and 1983.

The CCAR has continued, during the past 25 years, to issue resolutions or policy statements on issues of social justice and civil liberties, on world affairs and those within the Jewish community. One major statement was issued by the Committee on Church and State in 1965, another by the Committee on Judaism and Medicine in 1964. Many conventions deliberated the CCAR's views on Israel, especially after the Six-Day War of 1967 and Israel's assumption of the administration of Judea and Samaria. The Conference was equally active in voicing its concerns for oppressed Jewries (and non-Jewish communities at risk) throughout the world — from the Soviet Union to South Africa, from Central America to the Jewish and other minority communities in Arab lands. As resolutions adopted by the CCAR have been circulated each year to governments, agencies, associations, and individuals working in the subject areas, the CCAR has become a recognized and respected Jewish voice, and has often been consulted by these same agencies or by the media for its views as new issues have arisen.

Yet the greatest debates and the most troubling issues facing the Conference have not been external, but those involving rabbinic practices and Jewish status.

Although Eugene J. Lipman describes the issue of mixed marriage and rabbinic officiation elsewhere in this volume (p. 45), it is addressed here as an example of the attention devoted to a crucial subject over the course of many years. The essential re-affirmation in 1947 of a stand first adopted in 1909 — that mixed marriage is contrary to Jewish tradition, and therefore rabbinic officiation ought to be discouraged — did not lay the matter to rest. It remained a subject of rabbinic interest and discussion throughout the 1950s and 1960s, until in 1971 then-President David Polish called for a committee to report at the 1972 convention on the question of rabbinic officiation. A major, often emotional debate occurred, which was repeated in 1973 on the occasion of the presentation of a resolution. Once adopted, fears that the Conference might impose sanctions, and disaffection with what some rabbis saw as an ideological move to the right led a significant minority to form something of a caucus within the Conference, an "Association of Progressive Reform Jews." Rabbinic officiation remained on the Conference agenda for several years to follow.

At the end of the 1970s, the New England Region of the CCAR added to the debate with its call for expulsion of members of the CCAR who co-officiate at mixed marriages with clergy of other faiths. A special committee took up the question and in 1982 brought to the convention a new resolution "repudiating" the practice. The resolution was adopted. This in turn led to more serious discussion of sanctions, a question that was referred to the CCAR Committee on Ethics.

The Committee on Ethics found, after several meetings, that it was unable to arrive at an objective definition of "co-officiation," as a prerequisite for deciding when sanctions might be invoked. More seriously, the Committee on Ethics concluded that to invoke sanctions against those rabbis who co-officiate might imply endorsement of rabbinic officiation at mixed marriage ceremonies without co-officiation. Yet another committee, the *ad hoc* Committee on Rabbinic Standards, addressed the issue in an effort to resolve the impasse, but in 1985 they reached essentially the same conclusion and the matter was dropped.

The history of Conference consideration of the status of children of mixed marriage is not quite so long, but does trace its origins to the report of the Special Committee on Mixed Marriage and Intermarriage presented at the Montreal Convention of 1947. The report, accepted by the Conference, provides that in the event of a mixed marriage, a child of a non-Jewish mother is to be considered Jewish if (1) the parents declare their intention to rear the child as a Jew, and (2) the child is confirmed at the end of a religious school course. This was reflected in the 1961 edition of the *Rabbi's Manual*, which renders the opinion that parental intent and Jewish upbringing suffice, without conversion, to establish a child's Jewish identity in the event of a mixed marriage.

In 1976, the Committee on Conversion reviewed these provisions and in its annual report suggested certain changes in them, primarily relating to the basic educational requirements that a young person would have to fulfill to have his or her Jewish identity secured. By 1978, the Committee on Conversion moved to the drafting of a potential resolution, when the process was joined by the UAHC through a call from its president, Alexander M. Schindler (1979), for the CCAR to endorse a non-lineal descent resolution. The first full convention consideration of such a resolution came in 1980, when the Committee on Conversion's draft was referred first to the Committee on Responsa, then to an *ad hoc* Committee on Patrilineal (*sic*) Descent. A long debate ensued at the 1982 convention, and yet again in 1983 when the resolution was finally adopted.

Just as the Committee on Conversion began developing the CCAR's stand on Jewish descent, in 1976, another issue arose that remained unresolved for 14 years. That year the Conference first received a proposed resolution on homosexuality, relating specifically to the civil and criminal rights of homosexual persons. The matter was referred to a special committee that developed a resolution for presentation to the convention in 1977; the convention adopted a limited statement against the abridgment of civil and criminal rights, but the committee had been unable to formulate a broader statement on homosexuality itself, and dropped a draft paragraph before presenting its text to the convention.

The issue surfaced again in 1986 with the presentation of a draft resolution by a rabbi and a rabbinic student concerning the issues of admission to the HUC-JIR and to the CCAR, placement, professional standing of homosexual and lesbian rabbis, and the phenomenon of homosexuality. An *ad hoc* Committee on Homosexuality and the Rabbinate deliberated for four years, arranging interim convention discussions, the publication of papers, and discussions within most of the CCAR regions. The revised document, now a substantial position paper, was adopted at the 1990 convention.

Related to issues of Jewish descent and mixed marriage is the subject of Outreach, first proposed by the CCAR's Committee on the Unaffiliated in 1973. In that year the committee called for the CCAR to publish a manual for proselytes and recommended "that some kind of ongoing 'family-adoption' program be established in congregations so as to facilitate the convert's feeling of acceptance within Judaism and Jewish life." The formerly *ad hoc* committee became a standing Committee on the Unaffiliated, which in 1974 renewed its calls for a congregational outreach program with the UAHC. A joint commission with the UAHC was finally created by action of the CCAR Executive Board and the UAHC General Assembly in 1983. The movement's Outreach program has since become, through the joint commission and the UAHC Outreach Department, one of the major programmatic operations of Reform Judaism.

Ethics and Rabbinic-Congregational Relations

Just as the developing resolutions, responsa, position papers, and guides to Jewish practice contributed to the cohesiveness of the movement even in the midst of its diversity, so too did a growing body of internal procedures and guidelines seek to guide relations among rabbis and between rabbis and congregations. Disciplinary procedures also became more detailed during this period, along with the willingness to use them.

The first rabbinic Code of Ethics, for example, adopted in 1926, contained guidance for rabbi-rabbi and rabbi-congregation relationships but made no mention of disciplinary procedures. A revised code, in 1964, was less than a third the size of its successor, adopted in 1975, and merely stated that violations would be "dealt with" in accordance with the judgment of the committee, or referred to the Executive Board for disciplinary action. The section on "Suspension and Expulsion" in the 1975 code exceeds the entire length of the 1964 edition, and was to be expanded yet again at the centennial with consideration of another revised edition.

The Committee on Ethics found it relatively easy to respond to allegations of rabbis against their colleagues on issues of commercialism, occupying other rabbis' pulpits, or officiating without consultation at life-cycle events for those belonging to colleagues' congregations. More difficult were cases of lay complaints against rabbis or cases in which the committee had learned of transgressions — members advertising their services, for example — without having received a formal, written complaint. Most difficult of all were allegations of moral or sexual impropriety; these were not touched by the Ethics Code at all except by general reference to the need for "high ethical conduct by the members" (1975). The committee's inability to formulate guidelines or principles covering such cases led at times to frustration at being unable to consider serious instances of moral or ethical lapse. In 1964, then-President Leon Feuer called in his annual message for appointment of a Committee on Rabbinic Standards that would consider questions of rabbinic morality. Such a committee was appointed, in cooperation with HUC-JIR, and met four times in its first year. Conclusions of the committee were published in the 1965 *Yearbook* and cover rabbinic seminary training and ways to bolster moral behavior among rabbis. The report noted that lapses were apparently rare and allegations few, but no less important for the seemingly low rates of incidence.

The issue was also addressed in 1971 by the joint Presidential and Vice-Presidential message of Roland B. Gittelsohn and David Polish. They recommended that a special committee be appointed to deliberate on rabbinic conduct and attitudes, and to explore tenure and rabbinic "effectiveness," as well as the strengthening of the Joint Conciliation Commission. They also suggested, as part of the same process of lending weight to the movement's guidelines, the incorporation of "Suggestions for Procedures in Rabbinic-Congregational Relationships" into rabbinic contracts (see below).

The question of rabbinic morality, beyond specific provisions of the Code of Ethics, continued to concern the committee, and led in 1987 to the formation of a new committee devoted solely to the subject, the *ad hoc* Committee on *Kedushat Harabanut*. This committee examined codes of ethics and professional behavior from other religious and professional societies, including their procedures for receiving and considering cases of alleged misconduct. Many of these recommendations were incorporated into a draft revision of the code, to be brought to the Conference for a vote in 1991.

A formal structure to guide rabbinic-congregational relations was created in 1957, seven years before the Placement Office became an effective instrument of fair dealings between rabbis and congregations. In 1957 the General Assembly of the UAHC endorsed guidelines entitled "Suggestions for Procedures in Rabbinical-Congregational Relationships." A National Conciliation Commission, formed in 1959, has provided mediation and conciliation when problems arise between congregations and their rabbis. Renamed the National Commission on Rabbinic-Congregational Relations in 1973, the commission revised its guidelines in 1969, 1975, and 1984. These guidelines, together with the Rabbinic Code of Ethics and particular guidelines pertaining to placement ethics (1968) and placement procedures, have provided more stability to rabbis and laity alike. Despite an occasional gripe that the movement's guidelines are too restrictive or simply too numerous, it is likely that members of the CCAR enjoy better job protection and are better compensated than their counterparts outside the Reform movement.

Rabbis ordained outside the Hebrew Union College-Jewish Institute of Religion continue to apply for membership in the CCAR. Perhaps they are attracted by the high professional standing of our members. Although never constituting as many as 10 percent of Conference membership, such rabbis have applied who were ordained at Leo Baeck College in London, the Jewish Theological Seminary, the Reconstructionist Rabbinical Seminary, or occasionally, an Orthodox yeshiva. Given the great divergency in standards represented by the various seminary programs, the CCAR voted in 1980 to adopt admissions standards for the guidance of the Committee on Admissions. These standards grant standing equivalent for ordinees of Leo Baeck, the Jewish Theological Seminary of New York, and the now-defunct Reform rabbinical seminaries of pre-War Europe, but provide for a three-year probationary period for all but the graduates of Leo Baeck College. Those ordained elsewhere may be required to pass examinations. Private ordination is now an irrevocable barrier to CCAR membership, as is ordination by unaccredited seminaries.

Placement and Pension

The two most visible areas of Conference activity during the past quarter-century were placement and pension services. Placement has been of concern to members of the CCAR almost since its inception: in 1900 the president of the CCAR objected to the trial sermon, and first consideration of a proposed Pulpit Bureau appeared on the CCAR agenda in 1907. It was not until 1950, however, that the CCAR presented a placement plan to the UAHC for approval, a proposal defeated the following year. Thereupon, a provisional placement committee was created representing the UAHC, CCAR, and HUC-JIR but without the services of a full-time director.

The Conference presented a second plan in 1961, which was finally adopted in 1963 after vigorous debate within the Conference and the Union. Malcolm H. Stern became the first director in 1964, and established most of the procedures still effective today. Agreement on the plan had become possible after the CCAR agreed, among other things, to pay all expenses of the placement office and its director, and after agreeing as well that internal rabbinic placements within the UAHC and HUC-JIR would not have to be accomplished through the CCAR placement office or according to its guidelines.

Under its directors, Malcolm H. Stern (1964-1980), A. Stanley Dreyfus (1979-1991), and Arnold I. Sher (1990-), the Placement Commission has provided placement and counseling services for the members of the CCAR, established a guideline of placement ethics, adopted a system of congregational classification and guidelines for eligibility, created rules for in-house promotion, and provided contract guidelines and advice.

Coincidentally, in 1907, the same year as the first Pulpit Bureau proposal, consideration was given to the establishment of a pension plan for rabbis, but again, much time was to elapse before the creation of a viable program in 1943.

The Rabbinical Pension Board was created in 1943, with representation from the CCAR, the UAHC, and (later) the National Association of Temple Administrators and the National Association of Temple Educators. The original plan called for individual retirement income policies with a fixed death benefit to retirement, and a guaranteed income annuity at the age of retirement.

Premiums were set at 10 percent of the salary of the rabbi, with seven percent to be contributed by the congregation and the remaining three percent by the rabbi. The goal, of course, was to enable rabbis to retire in dignity and to retain mobility during their active years by participation in a system common throughout the movement.

Starting in 1956 the Rabbinical Pension Board began to study the feasibility of creating a true group retirement plan, a process that resulted in adoption of a group program in 1961. The same 10 percent contribution level was maintained, but the board was able, on a group basis, to purchase more insurance and larger annuities. The new plan also called for group insurance for the individual at a level of three times annual salary (with a $40,000 limit).

It quickly became apparent, however, that the 10 percent level of contribution would no longer suffice to ensure an adequate retirement, or to provide adequate pre-retirement death benefits from the insurance portion of members' contributions. Accordingly, the plan was amended to provide a 15 percent contribution, raised again in 1967 to 18 percent, with the goal of providing retirees with a pension of 60 percent of average annual salary as computed during the five years preceding retirement.

Over the years, the Rabbinical Pension Board has also administered a long-term disability insurance program, and, for some years, a health insurance program. The latter was terminated in 1985 because of unacceptably high rates.

The board makes available a number of retirement options, including various types of annuities and estate and lump-sum provisions. As the CCAR centennial approached, the RPB was adding to its agenda financial planning and retirement planning, and had begun to sponsor workshops at the CCAR conventions. The Rabbinical Pension Board held nearly $65 million in its variable equity fund, nearly $90 million in guaranteed investment contracts, and several million more in a fixed income portfolio. The plan served nearly 1,500 participants, providing benefits at a given time to more than 200 retirees.

Relations with Other Organizations

Given the extent of Conference programming described above, it is not surprising that the CCAR has continued to develop a network of cross-representation with other bodies, both within and outside the Reform movement. The closest ties remain, as they have since the CCAR's inception in 1889, with the Union of American Hebrew Congregations and the Hebrew Union College-Jewish Institute of Religion. Despite all of the diversity within the movement, virtually all HUC-JIR ordinees have continued to join immediately after ordination, and most full-time congregational rabbis have served Reform-affiliated congregations. Much of the movement's policy-making and programmatic offerings are derived from joint UAHC-CCAR commissions, including Education, Social Action, Rabbinic-Congregational Relationships, Outreach, Religious Living, and Synagogue Management, while Placement has included a joint partnership with both the HUC-JIR and the UAHC. The UAHC and CCAR executive bodies have had full cross-representation; the Rabbinical Pension Board, as described above, has been a joint operation of the CCAR, UAHC, NATA, and NATE.

Another joint program of the CCAR, UAHC, and HUC-JIR was created in 1984, with the formation of a *Berit Mila* program under the aegis of a *Berit Mila* Board. The program provides standards and courses for physicians who are then certified as ritual circumcisers.

Another joint body, the Association of Reform Zionists of America, also includes official representation from the CCAR, the UAHC, and its affiliates. ARZA was first proposed in March 1977, at a meeting of the UAHC Executive Committee. The project was endorsed by the CCAR Executive Board a month later, when the board rejected a proposal for Zionist affiliation through the American Zionist Federation, rather than through the movement's own body directly affiliating with the World Zionist Organization. The partnership with the UAHC in creating ARZA was cemented with the overwhelming approval of the 1977 CCAR convention.

The CCAR has continued its participation as a constituent agency of the Synagogue Council of America, the Conference of Presidents of Major American Jewish Organizations, and the World Union for Progressive Judaism; official representatives have also been appointed to the American Schools for Oriental Research, the National Conference on Soviet Jewry, the Jewish Chaplains' Council, and half a dozen others, while the Conference has supported — since 1978 — Religion in American Life, a vital association of all the major religious bodies and corporate executives. Joseph B. Glaser served RIAL as its chair for most of this period.

The CCAR also began an important dialogue with like-minded people in the Israel kibbutz movement, starting in 1971 with a three-day conference at Oranim (see the *CCAR Journal*, Winter 1973, for a full exposition of this conference). The dialogue continued periodically in conjunction with Israeli conventions of the CCAR; after the 1988 convention selected rabbis met with kibbutz and academic leaders at Beit Berl for a symposium on festival worship and practices.

Long-Range Planning

The increasing complexity of the CCAR, both structurally and programmatically, as well as the growing diversity of CCAR membership, has made clear the need for long-range planning and a study of the membership to ascertain their perspectives on every aspect of their work as Reform rabbis.

In 1964 President Leon I. Feuer appointed Eugene J. Lipman to chair an *ad hoc* committee to explore "the possibility of completely overhauling, modernizing, and hopefully simplifying our Conference structure, the committee set-up, and the convention agenda." The committee reported in 1965, and its recommendations on those issues were adopted. Two years later, in 1967, in an effort to serve the membership better, the Committee on Rabbinic Training proposed "a comprehensive study of the rabbinate within the context of a changing world, as well as a radically changing synagogue, Jewish community and Judaism itself." The study was approved by the board in 1968, after a separate Committee on Rabbinic Status urged the undertaking, which was also supported by President Levi Olan that year in his presidential address to the convention. The board sought the cooperation of the UAHC and HUC-JIR in 1969 by asking them to refrain from major fund-raising activity so that the Conference might raise the $60,000 to $80,000 needed for the project.

The study, under the direction of the renamed Committee on the Future of the Rabbinate and the Synagogue, was entrusted in 1970 to Dr. Theodore I. Lenn, professor of sociology at Connecticut State College. Dr. Lenn spent two years interviewing hundreds of rabbis. The resulting study became known as the "Lenn Report," and was presented to the board in 1972. Several of the major Conference programs described above derive from the conclusions reached by the study.

Continuing the process of study and planning, a new Long-Range Planning Committee was named in 1980 to study the Conference's relationship to its members and to recommend necessary structural and staffing changes. A report that called for a restructuring of the committee system, regions, and representation on the Executive Board was submitted to the 1983 convention but the proposals were rejected. A renewed effort was undertaken by the committee in 1989, starting with a new inquiry into membership demographics and concerns. As its first recommendation to the Executive Board, in 1990 the Long-Range Planning Committee proposed a major new study of the Reform rabbinate, suggesting a five-year time frame for design, surveying, and analysis. The board approved the proposal, hoping that the results of the new study would prove of substantial value to the CCAR as it enters its second century.

Centennial

As the CCAR approached the 100th anniversary of its founding, a special Centennial Committee was appointed to review the history of the CCAR, to plan for the observance itself, and to look to the future. This volume derives partly from that committee's work.

The Centennial Committee decided that the most appropriate observance should not be merely ceremonial, but should be primarily educational in nature, as it sought to share the work, achievements, and concerns of the Conference with its own members and with the larger community. A centennial film, *Rabbi*, was co-produced with the HUC-JIR; an essay competition was sponsored through the North American Federation of Temple Youth; a special Shabbat was designated; appropriate sermonic and educational materials were produced; and preparations were made of a Centennial *Yearbook* Index. Also such celebratory events as a community banquet at the Cincinnati convention, a centennial convention photograph, and the production of a comedic *Shpiel* all brought the CCAR into a greater public awareness and sought to instill renewed pride among its members.

One early suggestion to the Centennial Committee was not accepted: the preparation of a "platform" such as those adopted by Reform rabbis in Pittsburgh in 1885 and by the CCAR in 1937. The committee reviewed the work of a task force which had hoped to produce a platform-like statement on the 1975 centennial of the Hebrew Union College-Jewish Institute of Religion, but which had been forced to stop short of that goal, realizing that the ever-increasing theological and ideological diversity of its members would make adoption of an all-embracing platform impossible. The CCAR did adopt in 1976 a lengthy statement on Reform theology entitled "Centenary Perspectives," which celebrated diversity while couching its conclusions in more ambiguity than the true platform statements of earlier years. But the Centennial Committee expressed no unhappiness over the impossibility of adopting a platform. As the Conference prepared to enter its second century that very diversity that characterized the Central Conference of American Rabbis appeared to presage, not an era of weakness, but one of new strength for the Reform movement and its rabbinate.

TANU RABBANAN:
OUR MASTERS HAVE TAUGHT US

Eugene J. Lipman

The multi-faceted history of the Central Conference of American Rabbis can be approached through many doors. The one chosen here consists in the first instance of the annual messages of Conference presidents and the responses of the plenary body to those messages. From the beginning, major issues have frequently been raised, illuminated, and advocated by Conference leaders. Then they have been molded into policy positions through the committee processes, finally adopted by the annual convention to be put into action out in the world or incorporated into the procedures of the Conference.

Some issues have required the appointment of *ad hoc* committees to explore them in detail and to formulate draft positions for plenary consideration. (The first such, back in the 1890s and chaired by Isaac M. Wise, dealt with the circumcision of converts.) More frequently, as the committee structure of the CCAR proliferated, relevant committees wrestled with issues for presentation to the convention. In the handling of all issues, the democratic process has been consistent, albeit cumbersome at times.

Authority vs. Pluralism

After Isaac M. Wise was forced to give up his dream of a united American rabbinate transcending a spectrum of convictions regarding Judaism, he concentrated on a united Reform rabbinate, with authority. Almost from the beginning, he wavered on the authority question, but he tried.

In 1891: "We are the American Beth Din, with all the duties, rights, and privileges which the ancient expounders of the law secure to Beth Din." In the face of the "Eastern radicals" — Einhorn, his sons-in-law Kohler and Hirsch, and others — Wise did not hesitate to invoke the traditional powers of the Mei-a Rabbanim, 100 rabbis, when the membership of the Conference approached that number. He also emphasized the traditional uses of *gezeirot, takkanot*, and *seyagim*, and commended them to the emerging CCAR.[1]

In 1892: "In order to establish and perpetuate union among our co-religionists we must teach the young what we call sound doctrine." He proposed a "union school catechism" as well as a "union manual of worship." Both had to be preceded by a systematic theology, a document he had already prepared. A committee of five was appointed to edit such a volume.[2]

In 1894:

> The Central Conference at once rejects all illiberal elements and stands only and exclusively for the American Israel ... the very people that naturalized Judaism in America. The liberal principle and the reformatory practice are the *conditio sine qua non* for membership in this Conference.

Wise's determination to give to the CCAR authority over its members and over the Reform community was real. For example, in 1896 he sharply criticized the New York Board of Rabbis for authorizing on its own some liturgical music. This, he insisted, was the sole prerogative of the CCAR.

In 1919, on the 100th anniversary of Wise's birth, President Louis Grossman illuminated two aspects of early concentrations in the convictions of the CCAR's founder and his colleagues.

First was the passionate American patriotism of Wise and his colleagues and the deep feeling that Americanism, as they saw it, and Judaism, as they saw it, were deeply linked. Grossman said: "We represent what is historically true and that which neither radicalism can foist nor reactionism pervert." American Reform Judaism had made Judaism American, whereas German Reform had "pathetically" approximated its environment but never merged into it. "German Reform re-formed; it did not reform." American Reform has "purged us of every trace of alienism."[3]

Grossman went on: "American liberty and American Justice and the genius of American life are identical with Jewish verities and Jewish aspirations."[4] That view was widely held and preached by Reform leaders from Wise to Kohler to Morgenstern. Joseph L. Blau suggests that some went to "such extremes in identifying Judaism and Americanism that they are almost embarrassing to read."[5]

President Grossman also explicated in some detail the theology of Isaac M. Wise. It was expected that his colleagues shared his views and taught them as "official."

Wise was totally theistic. He accepted the Mosaic origin of the entire written Torah and the direct divine inspiration of the Decalogue. Wise accepted Maimonides' *Thirteen Principles*. For him, and apparently for his contemporaries in the CCAR, there were dogmas in Judaism: the existence of God as Persona with will, revelation, the requirement to worship, conscience (*sic!*), ethics, esthetics, immortality, and rewards and punishments.

Wrestling within the leadership of the CCAR over authority versus pluralism in principle and practice can be symbolized by two statements of Rabbi Wise's successor, Joseph Silverman. In 1901, President Silverman decried talk of consistency among Conference members. "The CCAR," he said, "is a common meeting ground for representatives of shades of belief and practice. It is an arena for combating heresies and testing new theories. It is a great clearing house of Jewish thought."

Two years later, Silverman proposed the creation of a permanent joint CCAR-UAHC synod which should make law regarding belief and practice for Reform Jews by a 75 percent vote of the two houses of the synod. President Joseph Krauskopf, in 1904, endorsed that proposal. Although there is no reported debate or discussion in the CCAR *Yearbooks*, the synod idea apparently brought on serious opposition. In his 1905 address, Krauskopf emphasized the pluralism of the Conference and no more was heard of a synod. But the tension between full pluralism and some measure of authority or discipline continued.

In 1923, President Edward Calisch called for the preparation of a major paper to be submitted to the Conference for adoption "that will be a formulation of the theology of American Judaism, and a statement of the principles in the light of the needs and the problems of the present day."[6] Instead, three major papers were presented at the 1924 convention, with the 100th anniversary of the founding of the "Reformed Society of Israelites" in Charleston, South Carolina, as the presenting reason. There was an extensive discussion re-evaluating the theoretical basis of Reform, its accomplishments, and its prospects.[7] There was no action.

By 1935, numerous suggestions had been recorded that a successor document to the Pittsburgh Platform was needed, even though that Platform had never been adopted as official by any Reform institution. The 50th anniversary of the Pittsburgh Platform presented a springboard for a massive series of papers on fundamental principles. Rabbi David Philipson, who had been secretary of the group that met in Pittsburgh and was its last survivor, detailed the background that had brought him and his colleagues to Rodef Shalom congregation in November of 1885.

Alexander Kohut had attacked Reform Judaism. Kaufmann Kohler had responded with a series of five addresses at his Temple Beth El, in New York. His congregation had published them, with a rather wide circulation. Kohler had then taken the initiative to invite his colleagues to a meeting in Pittsburgh to confer on his draft of Reform principles, resulting in the Platform.

Kohut and his circle had organized the Jewish Seminary Association in November 1886 as a direct result of the publication of the Pittsburgh Platform, according to Philipson.[8]

Professor Samuel Cohon's 1935 paper on God was a restate-
ment of classical theistic principles which differed little from Isaac
M. Wise's earlier writings. Rabbi Felix Levy's paper was not different in conviction, and is of interest primarily for his criticism of
the Pittsburgh Platform's lack of emphasis on the nature and
works of God.

Rabbi Joseph Rauch's paper on Torah emphasized progressive
revelation as crucial to an understanding of the meaning of Torah
in Reform Judaism. He believed that all previous revelations plus
an evolutionary covenant between God and Israel constitute
Torah.[9]

Nearly 100 pages were consumed by the two papers on Israel of
Rabbis Samuel Schulman and Abba Hillel Silver with subsequent
discussion and debate. They constituted a full exploration of every
facet of the conflict between Zionism and anti-Zionism that had
simmered and occasionally boiled within the CCAR beginning in
1897.

Two years later, the special Commission on Guiding Principles
for Reform Judaism submitted its report. A separate draft was
submitted by Schulman, a member of the commission who had
been ill and unable to participate in its deliberations. Because the
Columbus Platform of 1937 is the only official document of its
kind in the history of the CCAR, the process by which it was
finally adopted should be noted.[10]

A motion to receive the commission report and to consider it
seriatim was made. A substitute motion was made to send both
that draft and the Schulman draft back to the commission. Before
that could be acted on, a second substitute motion was made to
adopt no platform at all. The vote was 81-81, and the plenary
recessed for lunch. When the session resumed President Felix
Levy voted against the second substitute. The first substitute
motion was withdrawn. The original motion to receive the report
and consider it seriatim was adopted, 56-30. A motion to post-
pone action for a year was not adopted. After discussion, Rabbi
Philipson, as last survivor of the Pittsburgh meeting, asked for the
privilege of moving for the adoption of the Guiding Principles.
His motion was passed, but the breakdown of the 110 votes cast is
not recorded.

In his presidential address, Levy proposed that the adoption of
the Guiding Principles should be followed by the preparation of a
guide for ritual practices for Reform rabbis and congregations.
The President's Message Committee recommended that the CCAR
accept instead the results of a Synagogue Council undertaking to
publish all relevant resolutions of the CCAR and of its Committee
on Responsa. That recommendation was adopted by the plenary.

The dynamic tension between total autonomy/pluralism and some degree of discipline continued. In 1959, President Jacob Philip Rudin said:

> This is neither code nor guide, really, which I have in mind. It is the irreducible minimum upon which Reform Judaism must build. It is the foundation that I would see us lay. I do not ask that we determine how large shall be the house. I ask only that we discover how small it can be and still give all of us shelter. Surely there are such minimal standards. There must be. To say that there are not is to say that Reform Judaism is without its discipline for daily living. It would mean that there is no longer in Reform Judaism the binding strength of the People of the Book. We must preserve the word in our time, and in this time we must enlarge the word which is the law and the prophecy.[11]

Rudin recommended "that the will of the Conference be officially determined with reference to establishing minimum standards for Reform Judaism." The President's Message Committee responded by proposing that a committee be appointed to collate and publish past decisions of the Conference with regard to the principles and practices of Reform Judaism and arrange to submit such a text to the next convention for consideration and possible publication. It further recommended that the Commission on Jewish Education instruct its Adult Education Committee to arrange for the publication of a textbook on the principles and practices of Reform Judaism. The recommendations were adopted with no minimal standards.

In 1971, a new Committee on Guiding Principles was appointed. As it deliberated and debated it become clear that no document could be drawn that could possibly be adopted officially by the Conference. Instead, recognizing the 100th anniversary of the College-Institute, a centenary perspective was submitted to the 1976 convention. It was published in the *Yearbook* without comment. *A Centenary Perspective* is a detailed statement of Reform Jewish principles and approaches to practices following the Holocaust; the establishment of the State of Israel; the massive expansion of the Reform movement; the trends and tendencies within the movement's ideologies and practices; and, most clearly, the continuing pluralism and autonomy of rabbis, congregations, and individuals within Reform life.

Clearly, not all members of the CCAR are content. Rabbi Gunther Plaut may well have spoken for the less-than-contented in 1985 when he said:

We must confront the issue of autonomy and must begin with ourselves. ...
If and when we do this, people will cease asking about the authenticity of
Reform, and they will be much more open to this call than perhaps we even
dare to hope. Wherever our rabbis have attempted to proclaim it and have
done so with abandon and true dedication of time and effort, they have
been successful. Our people are ready; they are waiting for us.[12]

President Max Currick probably spoke truth when, in 1939, he
said, on the occasion of the 50th anniversary of the CCAR: "We
are not all of one mind on all questions, but in the cause of
Reform Judaism that unites us and does not separate us but joins
us to all Israel, we are one."[13]

Of differences, even stormy ones, Currick said:

They were differences for the sake of God, *l'shem shamayim*, and the
words of both sides were the words of the living God. It was out of these
conflicts that the achievements of the Conference were won and its contributions to the life of Jewry were made.[14]

The Bi-gendered Rabbinate

In the first generation of Reform Judaism in Germany, there
appeared to be broad agreement regarding the equality of men and
women in the synagogue. But there was no strong push for func-
tional equality of the genders, and certainly no attempt to train
women for the rabbinate. In Germany, Rachel Jonas did complete
studies at the Hochschule für die Wissenschaft des Judentums,
received private ordination, and served briefly as a rabbi before
her death during the Holocaust.[15]

In the United States in the early 1920s, having studied at the
Hebrew Union College, Martha Neumark requested ordination. In
1922, the CCAR endorsed the right of women to be ordained, as
did the faculty of the Hebrew Union College. The Board of Governors, which had referred the matter to the CCAR,[16] refused.

When Rabbi William Ackerman died in Meridian, Mississippi,
in 1951, his congregation requested that his widow Paula become
their rabbi. Paula Ackerman wrote to Dr. Julian Morgenstern,
president emeritus of HUC-JIR, for counsel. He responded that,
so long as she did not use the title "Rabbi" and so long as the civil
authorities gave her license to officiate at marriages, there was no
inherent reason for her not to lead the congregation. Paula Ackerman was called "Leader" of the congregation and served Beth
Israel without incident until she retired.

The matter came before the CCAR again in 1955, when President Barnett Brickner called upon the Conference to endorse the

ordination of women. A committee was appointed that reported in 1956 with a positive recommendation. The item was deferred for a year so that opposition opinion might be formally presented. The record is silent until 1972, when the admission of Rabbi Sally Priesand to membership in the CCAR is noted. What she faced can be symbolized by the following note in the Recording Secretary's report: "The following men were admitted to membership in the CCAR...," followed by the list including Priesand.

In her first presentation to the Conference, in 1975, Priesand made it clear that her acceptance within the CCAR had not brought on immediate and unanimous collegiality. "After all," she noted, "it may be another hundred years before the Conference again asks a woman to speak." Certainly, the first years were hard. In the Spring 1976 issue of the *Journal of Reform Judaism*, it was noted that increasing numbers of women were applying to the HUC-JIR to study for the rabbinate. In its next issue, the *Journal* spoke of "men" in connection with placement of rabbis, with no mention at all of women rabbis. The first article by a woman rabbi in the *Journal* did not appear until 1982. The CCAR Task Force on Women in the Rabbinate complained, with justification, about the paucity of female representation on CCAR commissions and committees. But, by 1988, there were women on every committee and commission, and a number of women had served on the Executive Board. As it celebrated its Centennial, the CCAR could point with pride to the status and accomplishments of about 150 members who are women.

Officiating at Mixed Marriages

Some of the early Reformers in Germany were very accepting of marriages between Jews and non-Jews and officiated at them. But that practice did not persist, not in Germany and not in the United States. To be sure, some well-known 19th-century American Reform rabbis did officiate at mixed marriages. Most did not. Kaufmann Kohler went even further. He would not permit mixed married couples to be members of his congregation — not the Jew or the non-Jew. He urged that position on his colleagues; he failed.

In 1909, the CCAR passed the following resolution: "The CCAR declares that mixed marriages are contrary to the tradition of the Jewish religion and should therefore be discouraged by the American Rabbinate."[17]

The subject was not discussed again by the Conference in plenary until 1947. Though it was maintained that few rabbis officiated at mixed marriages and then only under unusual circumstances, there was considerable discussion about strengthening the 1909 resolution to use the influence of the Conference to discourage rabbis from such officiating. A minority of the members were prepared to rescind the 1909 ruling altogether and leave the whole subject to individual rabbis. The debate was long and heated, according to the record. The "compromise" ultimately agreed upon was to renew verbatim the 1909 resolution.

The number of rabbis increased greatly over the following two decades; a disproportionately high number joined those who officiated at mixed marriages. By 1971 there was almost continuous debate at regional meetings and within individual synagogues and UAHC gatherings. Demands for a full review of the matter came from both of the rapidly-polarizing sides.

The matter came to the floor of the Conference in 1971 in the only message ever presented by a president and vice-president together. Roland Gittelsohn and David Polish discussed the subject at some length and then issued a joint statement as follows:

> We recommend that this Conference amend its historic statement (1909/1947) to read as follows: "The Central Conference of American Rabbis, having officially declared in 1909 and again in 1947 that Mixed marriages are contrary to the tradition of the Jewish religion, calls upon its members not to officiate at such mixed-marriage ceremonies."[18]

The President's Message Committee called for a full exploration of the subject for presentation at the 1972 convention, meanwhile reaffirming the historic position of the CCAR regarding mixed marriages.[19]

The exploration that took place in 1972 was certainly comprehensive. It consisted of a full evening of presentations, and most of a morning taken up with eight concurrent small-group sessions. The plenary adopted a resolution asking the *ad hoc* committee, chaired by Herman Schaalman, to bring concrete recommendations to the 1973 convention in Atlanta.[20]

The committee's report was presented in three parts. Part I added to the 1909/1947 resolution a call on CCAR members not to participate in mixed marriage ceremonies. Part II recommended that a rabbi who would officiate at mixed marriages refrain from doing so unless the non-Jew undertook a study course in Judaism; that such marriages not take place on Shabbat or festivals; and that no co-officiation take place with non-Jewish clergy. Part III urged that every attempt be made to have the children of such marriages raised as Jews and that every opportunity be made available to the non-Jew to convert to Judaism.[21]

Minority reports were heard from both polarities within the membership. Then, by agreement, one hour of debate was allotted to each of the sections of the report.

During the debate on Part I, an unprecedented letter, signed by 11 former presidents of the Conference, was read in favor of that section of the resolution. Part I passed by a vote of 321-196.

After full debate, Part II was referred to the relevant committees of the Conference by a vote of 221-198.

The final text of the resolution on mixed marriage, still in force in 1989, read:

> The Central Conference of American Rabbis, recalling its stand adopted in 1909 "that mixed marriage is contrary to the Jewish tradition and should be discouraged," now declares its opposition to participation by its members in any ceremony which solemnizes a mixed marriage.
>
> The Central Conference of American Rabbis recognizes that historically its members have held and continue to hold divergent interpretations of Jewish tradition.
>
> In order to keep open every channel to Judaism and K'lal Yisrael for those who have already entered into mixed marriage, the CCAR calls upon its members:
>
> 1. to assist fully in educating children of such mixed marriages as Jews;
>
> 2. to provide the opportunity for conversion of the non-Jewish spouse; and
>
> 3. to encourage a creative and consistent cultivation of involvement in the Jewish community and the synagogue.[22]

Lineality

It must be noted that the CCAR did not discuss, in a plenary meeting, the question of defining a Jew until the matter was referred to it by the UAHC in 1980. This occurred after UAHC President Alexander Schindler, at a Union General Assembly meeting, called for the Reform movement to define as a Jew the child of a non-Jewish mother and a Jewish father. In the 1947 extended debate on mixed marriage, the special committee (Solomon B. Freehof, Bernard Harrison, and Louis L. Mann) had stated categorically that the child of a non-Jewish mother is not a Jew. This statement had gone unchallenged throughout the debate.[23]

There is every indication that, for some decades, many Reform rabbis practiced a further recommendation of the same 1947 special committee. Infants could be considered Jews on the declaration of the parents to raise them as Jews. Such a declaration "shall be deemed as sufficient for conversion."[24] Older children, too, should not be subjected to any ceremony, but their education in religious school should take place, and Confirmation serve as the conversion service.[25] The 1961 edition of the *Rabbi's Manual* (p. 112) states this same position.

A Committee on Conversion (*Gerut*) first reported to the CCAR in 1978; it had a variegated agenda. At the 1980 convention, it presented a report that included a resolution on the status of children of mixed marriages.[26] The Conference determined to turn the issue over to a special committee, chaired by the vice-president, Herman Schaalman. The committee presented a report in "traditional" format: several papers representing varying viewpoints followed by long discussion. In his paper, David Polish reminded the Conference that the issue was not a new one at all, that in fact many members of the CCAR had been recognizing patrilineality for decades. It was, in his words, "the common law of our Conference."[27]

After long discussion, the plenary voted to return the matter to the special committee for further clarification. The report presented in 1983 included the resolution which, with amendments, was adopted by a large majority (more than three to one, though the actual figures are not reported in the *Yearbook*). Despite the fact that the resolution's preface states its applicability only in North America, there was strong opposition to it from MARAM (the liberal rabbinate of Israel). One focus of opposition from North American rabbis was the resolution's transformation of the basis of Jewish identity from the "ethnic" to the "confessional." The final resolution read as follows:

> The Central Conference of American Rabbis declares that the child of one Jewish parent is under the presumption of Jewish descent. This presumption of the Jewish status of the offspring of any mixed marriage is to be established through appropriate and timely public and formal acts of identification with the Jewish faith and people. The performance of these *mitzvot* serves to commit those who participate in them, both parent and child, to Jewish life.
>
> Depending on circumstances,[1] *mitzvot* leading toward a positive and exclusive Jewish identity will include entry into the covenant, acquisition of a Hebrew name, Torah study, Bar/Bat Mitzvah, and *Kabbalat Torah* (Confirmation).[2] For those beyond childhood claiming Jewish identity, other public acts or declarations may be added or substituted after consultation with their rabbi.

---

[1] According to the age or setting, parents should consult a rabbi to determine the specific *mitzvot* which are necessary.

[2] A full description of these and other *mitzvot* can be found in *Shaarei Mitzvah*.[28]

Few actions of the CCAR in its century of history brought on stronger reactions from a broader spectrum of individuals and institutions in the Jewish world. In 1987, when the standing Committee on Patrilineal Descent reported, however, its statement was brief, low-key, non-specific, and non-controversial. It indicated some "confusion," both within the Reform movement and in the larger Jewish community regarding the meaning of the resolution and its implications. It acknowledged the opposition that had arisen and stated that no change in the position of the CCAR was contemplated.

CCAR and UAHC

From the beginning, the CCAR and the UAHC have worked hard to achieve full understanding and harmony in function. Until World War II, there was a relatively sharp demarcation between the rabbinic members of the CCAR and the lay leaders of congregations who comprised the leadership of the UAHC. (During this period, rabbis on the miniscule staff of the Union in Cincinnati were known solely as "Mr."; they worked for a lay institution!)

Negotiations between the two institutions have covered a broad range of concerns — from allocation of tasks and areas of publication, to ideological matters, to the composition and functions of the many joint commissions and committees, task forces and *ex officio* Executive Board and Board of trustees members.

On a few occasions, more organic ties have been proposed. For example, in 1902, Rabbi Joseph Silverman proposed the creation of a joint UAHC-CCAR permanent synod. Early in the 1980s, a meeting of CCAR and UAHC leaders took place in San Francisco at which strong feelings were expressed by both rabbis and lay leaders regarding greater lay involvement in setting ritual policies for the Reform movement. (Traditionally, the UAHC General Assembly does not take on ritual policy-making.) There has been no further movement in that direction.

In both UAHC and CCAR meetings in the early 1940s, strong statements were made regarding the failure of Reform Judaism to capture the masses of American Jews. Reform was still a relatively small movement, with fewer than 300 congregations in the United States and Canada. In his 1942 message, President James G. Heller called for a joint conference of the UAHC, the CCAR, and the Reform seminaries (not yet united into HUC-JIR) to consider ways to transform our failures into a campaign to expand the horizons of Reform Judaism. Though the matter was transmitted to the Executive Board with a positive recommendation, there is no record of such a meeting having been called.[29]

It was the determination of Rabbi Maurice Eisendrath, when he became president of the UAHC, to break down the wall of separation between the institutions and leaders of Reform Judaism. The UAHC ceased to be a lay organization; it became totally a congregational body, and its policies were determined, at its biennial general assemblies, by laypeople and rabbis alike. Avenues of cooperation between the UAHC and the CCAR have continued to expand.

An occasional oddity is worth noting. In 1967, Temple Emanu-El of New York resigned from the UAHC in protest over Eisendrath's public statements. Both the fact and the substance of those advocacy statements were disapproved of by the congregation's leaders. The plenary of the CCAR supported Eisendrath's stance and called on Reform congregations to make up the monetary loss which accrued to the Union when Temple Emanu-El resigned.

As the Jewish Community Expanded. . .

The founders of the CCAR could not have predicted the size of the American Jewish community in 1990 or the uniqueness of the panoply of Jewish institutional life, in numbers of organizations, in scope of concerns (and duplication of functions), and in simultaneous coordination and competition. In 1890 there were few national Jewish groups: B'nai B'rith; the UAHC; the Board of Deputies of American Jews (later to be absorbed by the UAHC); the Hebrew Union College; the CCAR; and the Jewish Seminary Association, which would evolve into the Jewish Theological Seminary of the Conservative movement.

Over the decades, as Jewish institutional life expanded and became ever more complex, the CCAR consistently found its place and played its proper role. This role might be characterized on the one hand by an oft-expressed, almost wistful desire for a united Jewish communal structure in the United States. (The Canadian Jewish Congress has been functionally effective in that capacity since its inception in 1919, and has always included Reform congregations and national institutions.) On the other hand, the CCAR has been wary at times of joining in such alliances. The former tendency has dominated.

The earliest expressed position and action relative to a broad issue came in 1902. Concern was expressed regarding Jews traveling in Czarist Russia and their dangerous situation. Representative Goldfogle was working at a resolution from the House of Representatives on the matter. The CCAR favored his action.[30]

In 1903, President Joseph Silverman, reacting with deep passion to the Kishinev massacre, called for a central Jewish body because problems of such magnitude could not be handled in a fragmentized manner.[31] Movement in that direction was set back in 1906 with the formation of the American Jewish Committee and its immediate, powerful use of the clout of its leaders on Capitol Hill — many of them lay leaders of the Reform movement — who brooked no interference and sought no cooperation, least of all from rabbis. The same year, President Joseph Stolz deplored the fact that the American Jewish community had not been able to unite in response to the pogroms in Russia. He called for the continuation of the synagogue as the central Jewish institution, not to be submerged within secular Jewish groups.[32]

In a sense, the 1906 vignette is the story of the past 80 years: secular agencies, federations, umbrellas — which to join, which to oppose, which to ignore — thus it has been for the leaders of the CCAR. On more than one occasion the Conference replicated its action of 1917, when President William Rosenau called on the plenary to authorize joining the emerging American Jewish Congress, an umbrella at that time. The Conference voted not to do so.

There was an unusual series of internal debates beginning in 1920. After Prohibition became law, the Bureau of Internal Revenue (now IRS) issued regulations regarding licenses for "sacramental wine." They authorized the president of the CCAR, for example, to attest to the right of individual members of the Conference to sign applications for the distribution of such wine. In 1920 President Leo Franklin and Kaufmann Kohler wrote to the entire membership urging them to use, and to urge their congregants to use, unfermented "wine" and not to apply for licenses to secure fermented wine. There was apparently no protest or disagreement.[33]

A year later, abuses of the regulations were noted within the Orthodox community. A resolution was passed mandating the leaders of the CCAR to confer with the leaders of the Union of Orthodox Jewish Congregations about correcting those abuses. The resolution stated further that no CCAR member should sign any exemption authorizations for anyone.[34]

In 1917, a standing Committee on Cooperation with National Organizations came into being. It reported to the convention almost every year until 1931, after which it disappeared, with no explanation. The committee covered a broad spectrum of activities: cooperation with B'nai B'rith's Anti-Defamation League on stemming the rapidly-expanding anti-Semitism of the 1920s, work with a variety of organizations in opposition to the Immigration

Act of 1924, membership in and work with a national association
of religious liberals, and other contributions to a variety of national and international causes. It appears, however, that all these
relationships were tangential and almost incidental to the major
thrusts of CCAR operations — until 1925.

In his 1924 address, Rabbi Abram Simon discussed at some
length the negotiations to bring into being an international body of
Reform/Liberal/Progressive Jews. The proposal was referred to
committee.[35]

In 1926, the founding meeting of the World Union for Progressive Judaism was held in London. As part of his history-making
presidential address the year before, Simon had again urged the
CCAR to participate in the organization, and got consent. In fact,
17 members of the Conference attended that opening meeting. In
each generation of rabbis since, there have been men and women
who have labored faithfully with and for the World Union. In
general, however, one of the unfulfilled promises of the Reform
movement has been the non-centrality of the WUPJ in the
thoughts and actions of most members of the CCAR.

In that rich 1925 address, President Simon announced that, as a
result of his initiative, representatives of the congregational and
rabbinical institutions of "all shades of religious opinion would
meet in council to consider questions of Jewish unity of education
and of responsibility."[36] The meeting had been held in New York
— at the Harmonie Club, of course — and as a result the Synagogue Council of America came into existence. The CCAR has
consistently taken its proper place in the councils of the SCA,
even as Conference leaders have simultaneously regretted that it is
not an agency of real power and have joined its other constituents
in *not* regretting that this is so.

The Synagogue Council is a necessary institution as an opposite
number for the national Protestant, Roman Catholic, and emerging Islamic umbrella institutions and as a public forum in which
certain concerns of the Jewish religious community can be discussed and positions formed.

The existence of the Synagogue Council created an opportunity
for relationships among leaders of the three rabbinic bodies. In
1953, the first "private" meeting of the three presidents took
place. During the period from 1970-1990, periodic meetings of
presidents and executive vice-presidents occurred and were significant in trouble-shooting, prevention of tension, and approaches to
problem-solving. The peak public result of the periodic meetings
of the rabbinic leaders was a two-day conference in February
1988, held in Washington, D.C., on "Jewish Responses to Moral
Public Issues." It was sponsored by the Judaic Studies Committee

of George Washington University with the joint support of the CCAR, the RA, the RCA, and Washington's Foundation for Jewish Studies. The surmounting of all obstacles was due primarily to the assiduous work of President Jack Stern of the CCAR.

The relationships established and nourished in the rabbinic leadership meetings were most useful during the "Who Is a Jew?" controversy after the Israel elections of 1988. It can be assumed that the informal gatherings will continue.

Over the decades, there was a special and close relationship between leaders of the CCAR and leaders of the Rabbinical Assembly (Conservative). Periodically the presidents appeared at the conventions of the other body. In 1976, the CCAR approved a By-laws change making it possible for members of the CCAR to hold membership simultaneously in the RA. The reverse had already been made possible by the RA. At least 40 members of the CCAR held dual memberships.

After the success of the close cooperation between Reform and Conservative delegates to the 29th World Zionist Congress, President Ely Pilchik exultingly reported to the Conference:

> This cooperation of the Conservative and Reform Movements, this mutual respect, this trust and affection makes audible the echo of Deutero-Isaiah's: "*Harimi bakoach kolech m'vaseret Yerushalayim.*"
>
> I urge upon our Conference, our colleagues in their respective communities, the leaders of our 11 regions, and our national office continued and expanded cooperation with our Conservative colleagues in every area of endeavor. We cannot but win together.[37]

After the passage of the lineality resolution in 1983, relations between the CCAR and the RA became tense. The RA prohibited new joint memberships. After protracted negotiations, an agreement was undertaken to provide for "correspondent" relationships; that is, a member of either body can, by paying a small fee, receive the publications of the other.

The dynamic tension between the recurrent insistence of leaders of the Conference that the synagogue must be the dominant power in American Jewish life and the simultaneous insistence that the critical problems faced by Jewry required a united institutional approach continued after Nazism triumphed in Germany and as World War II approached. One polarity was trenchantly expressed by President Felix Levy in 1936:

> There are Jewish bodies in the United States that flout religion and flaunt secularism. Their leaders, and be it said to our shame and regret, have no "use" for religion or rabbi even when they support a congregation. What

right has anyone to be a director on a board of Jewish welfare or a worker in our philanthropic agencies, if he is opposed to Jewish education or if he believes that the Jewish religion has outlived its usefulness? ... Only the Jew sympathetic to Judaism and its religious values ought to be permitted to speak in its behalf, and not the rich, the powerful, or even the learned who are without this appreciation of and identification with religion.

I say we rabbis are partially to blame. We have not only tolerated this condition, we have abetted it. We associate in work with secular Jews and Jewish organizations and thus lend them our prestige and in a way give them our sanction. It is high time for us to tell the Jewish public, however strong or influential certain groups may be, that they need no longer look to us for cooperation if they are indifferent to our work and are neutral on, or opposed to, religion and the synagogue.[38]

At the same time, it became crystal clear to the leaders of the Conference that the unprecedented tragedy already engulfing European Jewry called for the transcending of all previous institutional rivalries. President Morris Newfield, in 1932, called for a world conference of Jewish leaders to discuss the European situation and to act resolutely. The President's Message Committee was less explicit: it proposed, and the convention approved, informal consultations among American Jewish organizations with regard to possible united efforts.[39]

The next year Newfield repeated his call for united action. He urged B'nai B'rith to take the lead. Failing that, he proposed that the CCAR do so. His proposal was adopted.[40]

In retrospect, there was a measure of naïveté in some of the statements by CCAR leaders during the years prior to World War II. One president was not certain that mass migration of Jews from Germany was the right answer! As late as 1938, President Roosevelt was commended for undertaking an international refugee conference, and the League of Nations for establishing a temporary commission on refugees — when it was quite obvious to most observers that neither undertaking had any reality in it.[41]

Much jockeying took place among national Jewish organizations. Finally, Henry Monsky of B'nai B'rith compelled the creation of the General Jewish Council, to whose first conference no rabbinical or congregational institutions were invited. In 1940, one representative of each agency was finally permitted, a "sop" to them as stated by President Emil Leipziger. There was major discussion at the CCAR convention about the democratization of the Jewish community, a far-from-infrequent subject within the councils of the CCAR. Nonetheless, the plenary voted to accept the invitation to serve in the Council. When it was succeeded by the American Jewish Conference, the CCAR took its place there and worked diligently through World War II.

The Conference became a member of the National (Jewish) Community Relations Advisory Council at its inception. In the early 1950s the NCRAC was rocked by what has become known as the MacIver controversy. Professor Robert MacIver of Columbia University had been commissioned to study the structure of Jewish community relations agencies in the United States and to recommend such changes in structure and function as would make this area of Jewish life more effective.

MacIver's detailed report created a furor. He recommended division of functions, with specific agencies specializing in specific tasks. In 1953, the issue blew up; the Anti-Defamation League of B'nai B'rith and the American Jewish Committee withdrew from the NCRAC, whose assembly had approved MacIver's proposals. President Joseph Fink of the CCAR, stated in 1953:

> We believe that the basic recommendations of the MacIver Report are factual and sound. The evidence which the report presents is convincing to the impartial mind. American Jewry should implement the recommendations of Dr. MacIver, rather than impede them. We regret that some of our national organizations whose policies are in conflict with the MacIver Report have withdrawn from the NACRAC. *Asu nevalah beYisrael*. Their withdrawal has been injurious and weakening to all American Jewry. It has made it obvious that more is needed in our national Jewish life than structural modifications; a new spirit is needed. This report has pointed the way to spirited cooperation among our national defense and other bodies; to follow a detour leading elsewhere is destructive of community spirit.[42]

His position was approved by the plenary.

Rabbi Fink insisted that the CCAR's position was, and must always be, motivated by Jewish religious concerns. Despite ongoing pressure from non-synagogue, non-rabbinical agencies to conform to their positions, positions backed by powerful lay leadership, much of it from Reform congregations, the Conference has consistently hewed to the line enunciated by Rabbi Fink in 1953.

Expressions of tension between the synagogue and the "secular" agencies of the American Jewish community have not abated. To the contrary.

In 1976, President Arthur Lelyveld described his perception of reality in trenchant terms. Since the Holocaust, he stated, the need to do everything possible for the She-erit Hapeleita, the survivors, has dominated Jewish life, including all efforts for Israel. Those efforts have centered in federations and welfare funds, whose leaders give and receive the ego-serving *kibbudim*, the honors so

lavishly distributed both in the American community and by
Israel's leaders. Rabbi Lelyveld called for a new partnership
between the synagogue and federation, a partnership to have the
synagogue serve as the wellspring for teaching and exemplifying
the Jewish values that produce and sustain leaders. If such a partnership cannot be brought into being, the synagogue faces the
danger of becoming more and more a "cultic, effete institution on
the periphery of the community, relegated to the life-cycle ceremonies."[43]

Rabbi Lelyveld recommended a joint study commission of the
CCAR and UAHC to look into synagogue-federation relationships
and into ways of developing leadership within and for the Reform
movement.

Two years later, President Ely Pilchik stated:

> To serve the welfare of the members of this Conference your leaders
> have agonized over the lack of progress in resolving our Synagogue-Fed-
> eration conflict. The problem grows. The Federations press harder and
> deeper. From all over the land we hear of increasing encroachment by Y's
> and Centers and Federations on the programs, and the activities, and the
> economic and human resources of the Synagogue. The burgeoning Fed-
> erations move toward relegating the Synagogue to something of an insig-
> nificant "shtibel" performing ancient life-cycle rituals highlighted by the
> "bar-baserei" of mitzvot primeval.
>
> The immediate past president of this Conference, that brilliant leader in
> contemporary American-Jewish affairs, Arthur Lelyveld, has taken on the
> responsibility of Chairman of our Joint Commission on the Changing
> Structure of the Jewish Community.[44]

Since Rabbi Lelyveld was simultaneously a leader of the Synagogue Council, strenuous efforts were undertaken for a joint declaration of the Council and the Council of Jewish Federations and
Welfare Funds. No such declaration was forthcoming. The
"commission" became a task force of the CCAR and UAHC,
which has no report in the record. The task of leadership development was given to a separate task force, which has worked diligently within the aegis of the Joint Commission on Synagogue
Management of the Conference and Union.

Zionism and Israel

In 1897, Rabbi Isaac M. Wise stated that all attempts to move
persecuted Jews to Palestine to help them set up agricultural and
other enterprises were laudable and the CCAR should lend maximum support to them. But, he continued, the problem was

politicians ... one of them called Dr. Herzl. ... We're not interested. We must counteract press reports about rabbis — some even attended the Basle Congress — and declare officially the American standpoint in this unpleasant episode of our history.[45]

The Conference overwhelmingly voted to oppose political Zionism; the UAHC followed suit one year later. At the same time, the CCAR and its leaders continued to support colonizing efforts in Palestine and the rehabilitation of The Land, even while continuing to illuminate the ideological conflict between Zionists and anti-Zionists at virtually every annual meeting.

A major confrontation took place in 1899. Professor Richard Gottheil, president of the Federation of American Zionists, enunciated the fundamental principles of Zionism:

1. Jews are more than a religious body, race (*sic*) and nation despite a lack of common home and common language.

2. A new home must be supplied if an end is to be made to Jewish misery.

3. Palestine is the only possible home. Not all Jews must return, however.

Rabbi Henry Berkowitz demurred on all three principles: The fatal error of Zionists is to believe that Jewish misery is permanent. It ignores that percentage of Jews who live in freedom and the trend toward a better life for more and more Jews. "Mankind has set its face resolutely towards a future of justice."[46]

Within the Jewish community, in country after country, resolute moves are being undertaken for more freedom. These movements are better than Zionism.

Jews must help themselves. This, said Berkowitz, is not the basis of Zionist work. Other nations must fulfill Zionism for it.

Finally, according to Berkowitz, being a religion is more significant than being a nation or a race. He then decried Gottheil's reference to race as a scientific blunder.

Rabbi Samuel Sale added: "To my thinking, Zionism is a dead issue; it is hardly a fad that is worthy of passing notice, for it seems to have its main support from those who have lost all feeling for and relation to Judaism." Judaism itself is "inherently universal. The status of Jews in the world has improved radically and will surely continue to do so. There is no need for Zionism."[47]

Professor Caspar Levias was to have participated in the debate, but was ill. He submitted a paper for inclusion in the *Yearbook*. He wrote: "The roseate view ... is due to various delusions." The classical mission of Israel can be carried out only from a home of our own. The stated anti-Zionist goal of "common humanity" requires either intermarriage, the breakdown of political boundaries, uniformity of ethical and religious ideals, or a combination of these. None of them is possible or even advisable. The popular slogan that "America is our Palestine and Washington our Zion" is called "patriotic hysterics" stemming from a fear of non-Jews.[48]

In 1901, Rabbi Joseph Silverman, successor to Wise, applauded Theodor Herzl's announced undertaking to persuade the Sultan of Turkey to approve of and to encourage Jewish colonization in Palestine. He urged that Herzl consult with an international conference of representative Jews to help him secure the two million pounds ($10 million) he called on the Jewish community to contribute for the colonization project.

The CCAR President's Message Committee, chaired by Sale, reported to the plenary its feeling that it would be inadvisable to cooperate with such an undertaking at that time. The Conference concurred, but requested that a paper on Jewish colonization be presented at the next convention.

The CCAR reacted to the Balfour Declaration of November 1917. President Louis Grossman's lengthy remarks on the subject were ambivalent. He accepted the sincerity of the British government's declaration and the potential for the enhancement of Jewish prestige as guardian of the Holy Land. But on the other hand, he did not consider such a declaration to be the way to achieve autonomy or independence. "No people has become genuinely free through somebody else." He emphasized the deep problems "a Jewish Palestine" would have with Christian Europe.[49] (He did not mention Islam!)

The President's Message Committee submitted the following statement, adopted by the convention after debate:

> The Central Conference of American Rabbis notes with grateful appreciation the declaration of the British Government by Mr. Balfour as an evidence of good-will toward the Jews. We naturally favor the faciliation of immigration to Palestine of Jews who, either because of economic necessity or political or religious persecution desire to settle there. We hold that Jews in Palestine as well as anywhere else in the world are entitled to equality in political, civil, and religious rights but we do not subscribe to the phrase in the declaration which says, "Palestine is to be a national homeland for the Jewish people." This assumes that the Jews although identified with the life of many nations for centuries are in fact a people without a country. We hold that Jewish people are and of right ought to be at home in all lands. Israel, like every other religious communion, has the right to live and to assert its message in any part of the world. We are opposed to the idea that Palestine should be considered THE HOMELAND of the Jews. Jews in America are part of the American nation. The ideal of the Jew is not the establishment of a Jewish state — not the reassertion of Jewish nationality which has long been outgrown. We believe that our

survival as a people is dependent upon the assertion and the maintenance of our historic religious role and not upon the acceptance of Palestine as a homeland of the Jewish people. The mission of the Jew is to witness to God all over the world.[50]

Consistent with the traditional concern of the CCAR for the development of Palestine, in 1924 President Abram Simon advocated the CCAR's involvement in the process of creating a non-political Jewish Agency for Palestine. The convention concurred, and in 1928 the Conference approved the program of the Jewish Agency.[51]

President Hyman Enelow, in 1929, stated:

The fact remains that Reform Judaism could not agree with the protagonists of the new Palestinianism, and thus it aroused their anger and hostility. So much the more eager, however, has been the desire of Reform Judaism to see Palestine treated as the Holy Land of the Jew and of the world, and to help to restore it as a place for Jewish people and as a habitation for the Jewish spirit.[52]

It should be noted that, in 1926, President Louis Wolsey (who would be one of the founders of the American Council for Judaism in 1943) issued a call which read:

I recommend that this Conference give its endorsement to the creation and establishment of a Liberal Synagog (*sic*) in Palestine, and that the Executive Board be empowered to appoint a Special Committee, whose responsibility it should be to develop a program and campaign in America and Europe for the realization of this purpose.[53]

The creation and establishment of Liberal synagogues in Palestine became one of the tasks of the newly-formed World Union for Progressive Judaism.

Immediately after the Nazis came to power, in March 1933, President Morris Newfield said, and the Conference confirmed:

The plight of German Jewry will force a large number, especially of the younger generation to migrate. ... The future of German Jewry seems hopeless. No wonder that in spite of their natural love of the Fatherland, large numbers will be compelled to find a new home. ... Palestine alone seems to offer possibilities for settlement of a comparatively large number. The Jewish Agency is taking steps to make such a mass-settlement possible. The Jews of the world are asked, or will be asked to raise funds for this purpose. Irrespective of our views on Zionism, American Jewry will respond to this appeal. I therefore recommend that the CCAR heartily endorse the appeal of the Jewish Agency for adequate means to promote the settlement of large numbers in Palestine, and that we urge the members of the Conference to support this endeavor in their respective communities.

The Conference expressed in strong terms its distress and chagrin over the 1939 British White Paper on immigration to Palestine. It asked the U. S. State Department to communicate to the British the CCAR's pleading that they keep the Balfour Declaration and other pledges to facilitate Jewish immigration.[54]

Even as the CCAR and its members expanded efforts for the rehabilitation of Palestine and the immigration there of European Jews, the inner conflict over Zionism as an ideology became exacerbated and bitter. The climax was reached at the 1942 convention in Cincinnati. A resolution introduced by 33 members of the Conference read in part as follows:

> And whereas the Jewish population of Palestine is eager to defend its soil and its home to the last man,
>
> And whereas, despite its formal approval of the plan, the Government of Great Britain has still failed to avail itself of the offer of the Jewish Agency for Palestine to establish a military unit based on Palestine. ...
>
> Be It Resolved, that the CCAR adds its voice to the demand that the Jewish population of Palestine be given the privilege of establishing a military force which will fight under its own banner on the side of the democracies, under allied command.[55]

The debate was long and heated. The arguments for different types of Palestinian Jewish units was confusing, but not central to the heat. It was Zionist versus anti-Zionist. A motion to table the entire matter and to expunge it from the record, to prevent trouble both inside and outside the CCAR, lost by six votes. The resolution, as reworded somewhat by the President's Message Committee, passed by a vote of 64-38.

That summer, a group of CCAR members met and organized the American Council for Judaism. Eventually, more than 90 Reform rabbis joined it. At the 1943 meeting, President James Heller pleaded eloquently and at great length for the ACJ to disband, in view of both the situation in Europe, and the near-hysterical reactions in the press and in the community. The convention itself took no action.

Inevitably, the collective mood of the CCAR was radically different when it met in 1946. In the middle of the convention, word was received of the arrest of the leaders of the Jewish Agency in Palestine and of hundreds of other persons in the Yishuv. Words such as "unconscionable," "shocking," "oppressive," and "tyrannical" were heard, and written into one of the most emotional resolutions the CCAR had ever produced, certainly on any subject related to Palestine. Rabbi David Philipson spoke of his "deep-seated horror." By this act, he said, Great Britain had forfeited all the respect and life-long love he had felt for her. He suggested that the resolution be presented directly to President Truman by a committee of three persons, one of whom he requested to be. The resolution and the direct presentation of it were approved.

To no one's surprise, the CCAR hailed the establishment of the State of Israel in 1948 and sent warm messages to President Weizmann and to Prime Minister Ben-Gurion. Rabbi Abraham Feldman's call for an end to debate over Zionism was responded to positively.

The last two decades of the CCAR's first century of life were punctuated by consistently positive statements and actions relative to Israel with frequent admixtures of concern about discrimination against non-Orthodox Jews and communities in the Jewish state. President Jacob Weinstein, in his response to the Six-Day War, urged his colleagues not only to accept Ambassador Ephraim Evron's challenge to lead their congregations in sending money to Israel and in using every possible political influence to support Israel's position, but also to send young people in a Peace Corps-type operation.

In 1969, the CCAR was the first Jewish institution to adopt Yom Ha-Atzma-ut, Israel's Independence Day, as a permanent religious festival to be observed on the 5th of Iyyar "as one of our spiritual and religious festivals." (The regulations of the Chief Rabbinate of Israel carefully do not use the word *chag*, festival, in connection with the 5th of Iyyar. See *Tikkun Yom Ha-Atzma-ut*, Jerusalem 1957, page 11). That decision was formally proclaimed on Mt. Scopus when the CCAR met in annual convention in Jerusalem in 1970. Some years later, the annual convention mandated that it meet in Jerusalem every seventh year. That schedule has been adhered to.

When the Association of Reform Zionists of America (ARZA) was established in 1977, with former CCAR president Roland Gittelsohn as its leader, the Conference enthusiastically endorsed the body and CCAR leaders have been actively involved in the expanding work of ARZA. Strong cooperation between the Reform and Conservative movements has resulted in strong resolutions for religious pluralism in Israel having been enacted at three World Zionist Congresses, despite determined and even violent opposition from Orthodox delegates.

Two aspects of the CCAR's involvement with Zionism and Israel must be emphasized.

First, Reform leaders have participated in a deep change in the meaning of the word *Zionism* and its implications. As do most American Jews, Reform Jews equate Zionism with pro-Israel convictions and actions aimed at the preservation and enhancement of the life of the Jewish people, not as an ideology about the nature of Jewishness.

Second, unlike most American Jews, CCAR members consciously and deliberately teach and live their brand of Zionism as *kodesh*, as a sanctity, as a major mitzvah in the undertaking to fulfill the life of mitzvot required of Jews. There is pressure on the CCAR to act as a political body within the World Zionist Organization, within the Jewish Agency, and in all relationships in Israel. It remains the conviction of the CCAR that it work as a Jewish religious agency in its various struggles in and for Israel. What is done, is done as a mitzvah.

Social Justice and Social Action

The first generation of Reform Jews in Germany re-established the ethical imperatives of Judaism as the peak of their aspirations. They used prophetic themes constantly in their sermons. The first generation of American Reform rabbis did the same. The early yearbooks of the CCAR are replete with magnificent oratory about prophetic Judaism.[56] Gradually, the CCAR and its leaders began to concretize their oratorical idealism.

The first specific action recorded was in 1904, when President Joseph Krauskopf called for, and got, a resolution opposing the teaching of religion in public schools.[57] Relationships between religion and the state occupied much attention of the Conference for decades. The relevant committee had a representative in every state to monitor state and local legislation and possible violations of the maximum separation of religion and state, the policy to which the Conference consistently adhered. Each Supreme Court decision viewed as positive by the CCAR was hailed. (e.g., Ill. ex re McCollum v. Board of Education, 1948, which banned religious teaching in public schools). Any decision viewed as eroding the "wall of separation" was decried.

Between 1965 and 1985 there was a letdown in the intensity of the CCAR's concern about religion-state issues. For a time, the committee was made part of the more general Committee on Justice and Peace. The emerging trend of erosion during the period of the "Burger Court," however, increased the sensitivity of many members of the Conference to the issue, and increasing emphasis was placed on it as the CCAR approached its Centennial.

By 1912, a number of other issues had been brought into the collective consciousness of the annual convention. That year President Samuel Schulman said:

What greater "Kiddush Hashem," what greater exaltation of the religion could there be than for Rabbis so to act, with courage and uprightness, as to win the confidence of both laborer and employer and be the makers of peace — but of a peace that is the only enduring one — the effect of "righteousness." I recommend that the name of the Committee on Synagogue and Labor be changed to that of "Synagogue and Social Justice," that its membership be enlarged, that it be understood that it is the Committee's duty to be ever on the lookout for an opportunity to improve the conditions of life for the masses of our brethren, to make for justice and humanity in industrial relations and to be ready to co-operate with all other national bodies or any other agencies that are engaged in the task of social reform, of interpreting the awakened social conscience and at the same time of vindicating those moral ideas of righteousness and justice, which are greater even than the material interests of men.[58]

The rights and problems of industrial labor, especially of women and children, was one of the two central concerns of the CCAR for many years. The Statement of Principles drafted by the committee in 1918 and approved by the plenary body in 1920 stands as a monumental achievement. It included a more equitable distribution of industrial profits; minimum wage; eight-hour day for all workers; government regulation to ensure safe and sanitary working conditions; abolition of child labor; workmen's compensation; universal health insurance; public employment offices; the right of labor to organize and bargain collectively; mediation, conciliation, and arbitration of labor disputes; proper housing for all citizens; mothers' pensions to preserve the integrity of the home; and constructive care of dependents, defectives, and criminals.[59]

Multi-issue social platforms were adopted subsequently by the CCAR in 1928, 1960, 1973, and 1983. None of them retreated from the principles of predecessors. They expanded the areas of concern of the CCAR and updated specific issues.

But the Conference did more than pass resolutions and promulgate liberal position papers. A peak period of active involvement in the world occurred in 1927. There was a strike of engineers and firemen on the Western Maryland Railroad. The strike had significance beyond the local because the railroad was only one of two Class A carriers which had refused to deal with the railroad unions. The Commission on Social Justice was asked to join with the Federal Council of Churches (now the National Council) and the National Catholic Welfare Conference (now the United States Catholic Conference) in investigating the strike. The recommendation was adopted by the plenary.[60] Rabbi Edward L. Israel of Baltimore represented the CCAR in the investigation and reported fully to the 1927 meeting. The report of this joint body was widely publicized and reprinted all over the United States. Its publication had been authorized by the plenary.[61]

There had been some joint action by the CCAR and the UAHC's social justice committee, but the Union pulled out in 1927. Any connection between the western Maryland action of the CCAR and the breakup of the joint enterprise is unclear. There were repeated calls by the CCAR for ongoing joint action (e.g., 1927, 1946). These would culminate in the formation of the Commission on Social Action of Reform Judaism in 1948.

The other great issue which occupied the CCAR in the arenas of social justice was international peace, both general and in specific instances. In 1928, a resolution was passed calling for the removal of United States troops from Nicaragua.[62] (The resolutions of the late 1980s about Nicaragua were different from this only in the absence of United States military forces in that unhappy little country. The CCAR disapproved vigorously of the American government's support of anti-government troops both with armaments and with "advisers.")[63]

The CCAR was consistent in its advocacy of peace and steps toward disarmament and international peace — in peacetime. As indicated earlier, the Conference was passionately patriotic during World War I. How much the more so was its involvement during the Second World War!

In the Spanish Civil War, the Conference was clearly on the side of the Republican forces. (It is of passing interest to note that, in light of the great sensitivity of Jews during that period to charges of pro-Communism, the reference to support for the North American Committee to Aid Spanish Democracy was deleted from the draft resolution.)[64]

The outbreak of the Korean "police action" provided the setting in which the Committee on Justice and Peace could approve the action because it was technically a United Nations undertaking. The CCAR could thus urge the United States government to use this opportunity to expand the role of the United Nations as an international authority and as "the nucleus of World Government."[65] That resolution was adopted.

In almost-violent contrast was the reaction of the Conference to the Vietnam War. In 1967, President Jacob Weinstein issued a stinging indictment of that expanding conflict. His statement had three parts: opposition to the war itself; insistence that the Reform movement still had an obligation to provide chaplains for Jewish soldiers; and conviction that the CCAR's traditional support for conscientious objectors to war (which dated back to World War I) should be expanded to include support of selective conscientious objection. This became Conference policy.[66]

The spectrum of CCAR concerns in the fields of social justice continued to be maximally broad, building on the great platforms of 1920 and 1928. In 1939, a resolution called for a detailed study of health-care needs of low-income groups including a full report. The first task undertaken by the Commission on Social Action of Reform Judaism was a national conference on health care. It was, in fact, the only action undertaken by the commission until 1953, when the UAHC took the initiative in staffing the Joint Commission. It expanded rapidly until it included every organized body within Reform Judaism: the CCAR; the UAHC; the National Federations of Sisterhoods, Brotherhoods, and Youth; and the National Associations of Temple Educators and Temple Administrators.

It would be impossible to catalogue all the issues dealt with by the CCAR in resolution and in action over its century of life. A few more should be noted, however.

The plenary resolved to favor "birth regulation" in 1930. That position was reaffirmed and strengthened in 1947 and went further, to urge Planned Parenthood services in hospitals and other public agencies.[67]

In 1967, the Conference adopted a resolution that accepted therapeutic abortion as "religiously valid and humane" under many circumstances, including the need to guard the emotional as well as the physical well-being of the mother. It urged "the broad liberalization of abortion laws in the various stages."[68]

An even more open, detailed resolution was passed in 1975, which included a call for support by both the CCAR and the UAHC of the Religious Coalition for Abortion Rights.[69] This resolution was reaffirmed in 1980, along with strong statements on the traditional Jewish basis for the abortion rights position.

Concern with immigration issues began relatively parochially when the United States Congress first began to consider immigration limitations after World War I. The CCAR opposed those limitations, and continued to work both independently and in immigration coalitions — for maximal immigration rights, against national quotas, and most strongly for changes in policy after World War II to make possible the entry of refugees (the major controversy over the Stratton Bill in 1946-1947). Vigilant concern in this area continues.

The CCAR has always favored the broadest interpretation of all clauses of the First Amendment to the United States Constitution. It has openly advocated support for the American Civil Liberties Union, and has generally agreed with the policy positions of that First Amendment defender. (Strong resolutions of support were passed after many Jews, angered by the ACLU's support of the right of American Nazis to march, with permit, in Skokie, Illinois, resigned from the organization.) Obviously, the Conference was strongly anti-McCarthy, condemning the Wisconsin senator roundly and rejoicing at his downfall.

The Conference has been equally unequivocal in its support of the civil rights movement. The Supreme Court decision in *Brown v. Board of Education* in 1954 was hailed by the CCAR, many of whose members had been in the struggle against segregation for many years. In 1956, President Barnett Brickner called for a summit meeting of Southern religious leaders of all denominations to unite in action. That meeting was not held. In 1961, President Bernard Bamberger hailed the Freedom Riders, almost without reservation. A concurring resolution was passed by the plenary.[70]

In 1963, a large delegation of CCAR members participated in the Interreligious Conference on Religion and Race in Chicago, which meeting played a major role in paving the way for the great March on Washington in August of that year. It is impossible to count how many members of the CCAR and their families participated in that outpouring of committed people and in many regional replications.

While the CCAR was meeting in 1964, a call came from Dr. Martin Luther King, Jr., asking for rabbis to come immediately to St. Augustine, Florida, where a major confrontation was brewing between segregationists and their interracial adversaries. Sixteen rabbis went that day, along with Albert Vorspan, director of the Commission on Social Action, who was attending the CCAR meeting. The group spent most of three days in the St. Augustine jail. The action received nationwide attention, as did many actions in the civil rights campaign in which rabbis participated along with a disproportionately-high-number of Jewish laypeople.

Affirmative action programs have been a thorny problem for all American Jewish organizations, primarily because of the shadowy boundary between affirmative action and quotas, a word and concept long-hated by Jews with historic memories. The shadows have not been removed by various complex and confusing Supreme Court decisions. The CCAR led a minority of Jewish institutions in stating that affirmative action "is an effective means of correcting historic injustice in our society."[71]

Economic issues have traditionally been among the most difficult for the CCAR to handle. They have always been most complicated and hardest to articulate. But the Conference has frequently tried to deal with the general question of economic rights
of all citizens. Poverty anywhere in the world has been anathema
to the members of the CCAR. In 1962, for example, it took a
strong position in favor of sending large quantities of food to
mainland China, which had suffered severe crop failures. It was
not a totally popular position, even during the Kennedy administration.[72] Not surprisingly, the Conference gave strong endorsement to the War on Poverty envisioned by President Kennedy and
announced by his successor. On a number of occasions, the
CCAR has deplored the failure of the U. S. government to take
that domestic war more seriously, allowing it to sink into relative
insignificance under the impact of the Vietnam War.

Due in large part to the strenuous efforts of West Coast rabbis,
led by Rabbi Joseph Glaser, later to become Executive Vice President of the CCAR, the organization gave strong support to the
United Farm Workers of America's battle for recognition, for
support, and for better conditions for western farm workers. It
endorsed the grape boycott[73] and later the lettuce boycott.

The CCAR viewed with alarm the ongoing breakdown of the
progressive income tax system. In 1969, it called for reforms "to
do away with the special privileges which have steadily eroded
our nation's faith in the equity of its tax system."[74]

The Conference has strongly supported all efforts for gender
equality in our society, including the Equal Rights Amendment.
The location of the 1979 annual convention was cause for controversy. After it had been scheduled — eight to ten years in
advance, as is necessary for a large convention — and all contracts had been signed long-since, Arizona turned up on the list of
states that had rejected the Equal Rights Amendment. Strenuous
efforts were made to cancel contracts, without success. The meeting was held in Phoenix and featured a major session on ERA;
non-ERA states were discussed in workshops; and Arizona legis-
lators were called on regarding the ERA.[75]

In recent years, alcohol and drug abuse, AIDS, and work with
AIDS patients and their families have received major attention
from the Conference.

After the 1961 establishment of the Reform movement's unique
Religious Action Center in Washington, a development approved
by the CCAR, the role of the Conference narrowed perceptibly in
the field of social action. The CCAR's representatives on the
Commission on Social Action did what was expected of them, but
the commission itself became less of an action group, with the

Religious Action Center occupying center stage brilliantly. Late in the 1980s, movement began toward greater involvement of individual rabbis around the country, of CCAR regional groups, and of the Conference itself.

In 1952, President Philip S. Bernstein declared:

> Reaction is on the march. Little men, frightened men, evil men would rob us of freedom in the name of freedom. Thought control, intimidation, guilt by smear and association are becoming more pervasive. Increasingly men are fearful to express themselves frankly on controversial issues. The long tentacles of repression are reaching into the schools and colleges, and are seeking to strangle the free press and to close the mouths and minds of legislators. Here the role of the liberal is plain — to resist this repression with clear mind and with undaunted heart.[76]

Nearly 40 years later, it can be said that some of the same kinds of forces are still at work in our society. But it must also be said that the men and women of the CCAR continue to respond as they did 40 years ago and for 60 years before that — as religious liberals.

It was this writer's high honor to serve as president of the CCAR during the Centennial year. At the end of my Centennial message, I said:

> We are known as a liberal organization. We are known as strong critics of many rightist trends in our society, trends in which Jews participate and even lead. We are accused of being knee-jerk liberals, of being unwilling to face the new realities, so-called, which are popular today both in the United States and Canada.
>
> We are in fact a liberal organization, and always have been. How can it be otherwise?
>
> Nowhere in the sacred literature of our people do I find justification for "me-first-ism" as a positive value for individuals. Nowhere in our sacred history since Mt. Sinai can I find buttressing for unfettered greed as a good thing for human society. Nowhere in our communal experience can I find a basis for believing that government is by nature an enemy of the people, except when our institutions are feeding at the public trough for our projects. Nowhere in the annals of Jewish history can I find extolled the erosion of the rights of all citizens, vengeful incarceration and the civil murder called capital punishment, the closing of borders to politically persecuted people. Nowhere in the commands of my *Metsaveh* can I find a mandate to continue discrimination against racial, ethnic, and other minorities in education, in housing, in employment. Nowhere in our writings about human relationships can I find approved the amassing of huge fortunes by a few while millions of individuals and families live on the streets, in automobiles, in hideous public shelters. Nowhere does my God

command the establishment of a permanent class of poor people doomed to leave the *yerusha* of their poverty to their children and to their children. Nowhere. I am a liberal because I am a religious Jew. This CCAR must be a liberal organization because we are and shall remain a Jewish religious group, bound to the Covenant we all swore to uphold at *Ma-amad Har Sinai.*

NOTES

1 *CCAR Yearbook,* 1892, p. 9.
2 *CCAR Yearbook,* 1893, pp. 28f.
3 *CCAR Yearbook,* 1919.
4 *Ibid.*
5 *Reform Judaism: A Historical Perspective* (KTAV, 1973), p. 12.
6 *CCAR Yearbook,* 1923, p. 107.
7 *CCAR Yearbook,* 1924, pp. 222-344.
8 *CCAR Yearbook,* 1935, pp. 193f.
9 *Op. cit.,* pp. 246ff.
10 *CCAR Yearbook,* 1937, pp. 94-114.
11 *CCAR Yearbook,* 1959, pp. 11f.
12 *CCAR Yearbook,* 1985, p. 10.
13 *CCAR Yearbook,* 1939, pp. 247f.
14 *Ibid.*
15 Michael Meyer, *Response to Modernity,* p. 379.
16 *American Reform Responsa* (CCAR, 1983), pp. 25-43.
17 *CCAR Yearbook,* 1909, p. 170.
18 *CCAR Yearbook,* 1971, p. 16.
19 *Op. cit.,* p. 51.
20 *CCAR Yearbook,* 1972, p. 91.
21 *CCAR Yearbook,* 1973, pp. 63-64.
22 *Op. cit.,* p. 97.
23 *CCAR Yearbook,* 1947, pp. 170f.
24 *Op. cit.,* p. 170.
25 *Op. cit.,* p. 171.
26 *CCAR Yearbook,* 1980, p. 37.
27 *CCAR Yearbook,* 1982, p. 72.
28 *CCAR Yearbook,* 1983, p. 160.
29 *CCAR Yearbook,* 1942, pp. 219-220.
30 *CCAR Yearbook,* 1902, p. 28.
31 *CCAR Yearbook,* 1903, p. 26.
32 *CCAR Yearbook,* 1904, pp. 230f.
33 *CCAR Yearbook,* 1920, p. 18.
34 *CCAR Yearbook,* 1921, p. 91.
35 *CCAR Yearbook,* 1924, p. 154.
36 *CCAR Yearbook,* 1925, p. 226.
37 *CCAR Yearbook,* 1978, p. 5.

[38] *CCAR Yearbook,* 1936, pp. 146f.
[39] *CCAR Yearbook,* 1932, pp. 126-127, 150.
[40] *CCAR Yearbook,* 1933, pp. 130f.
[41] *CCAR Yearbook,* 1938, pp. 167f.
[42] *CCAR Yearbook,* 1953.
[43] *CCAR Yearbook,* 1976, pp. 6-7.
[44] *CCAR Yearbook,* 1978, p. 7.
[45] *CCAR Yearbook,* 1897.
[46] *CCAR Yearbook,* 1899, p. 169.
[47] *Op. cit.*
[48] *Op. cit.*
[49] *CCAR Yearbook,* 1918, p. 175.
[50] *Op. cit.*, pp. 133f.
[51] *CCAR Yearbook,* 1928, p. 140.
[52] *CCAR Yearbook,* 1929, pp. 172f.
[53] *CCAR Yearbook,* 1926, p. 144.
[54] *CCAR Yearbook,* 1939, p. 213.
[55] *CCAR Yearbook,* 1942, pp. 169f.
[56] Cf. Robert Kahn unpublished doctoral dissertation on liberal preaching by Reform rabbis in the 19th century. (HUC-JIR Library.)
[57] *CCAR Yearbook,* 1904, p. xx.
[58] *CCAR Yearbook,* 1912, pp. 251f.
[59] *CCAR Yearbook,* 1920, pp. 87f.
[60] *CCAR Yearbook,* 1926, pp. 106-107.
[61] *CCAR Yearbook,* 1927, p. 40.
[62] *CCAR Yearbook,* 1928, p. 139.
[63] *CCAR Yearbook,* 1986, p. 212.
[64] *CCAR Yearbook,* 1987, p. 151.
[65] *CCAR Yearbook,* 1951, p. 100.
[66] *CCAR Yearbook,* 1967, pp. 6f.
[67] *CCAR Yearbook,* 1947, pp. 219f.
[68] *CCAR Yearbook,* 1967, p. 103.
[69] *CCAR Yearbook,* 1975, pp. 70f.
[70] *CCAR Yearbook,* 1961, p. 146.
[71] *CCAR Yearbook,* p. 47.
[72] *CCAR Yearbook,* 1962, p. 142.
[73] *CCAR Yearbook,* 1968, p. 87.
[74] *CCAR Yearbook,* 1969, p. 100.
[75] *CCAR Yearbook,* 1979, p. 42.
[76] *CCAR Yearbook,* 1952, pp. 294f.

THE RABBI AS RELIGIOUS FIGURE

SAMUEL E. KARFF

The Changing Role of the Rabbi

Robert Bellah reminds us that

> religious institutions are social settings for the encouragement of the spiritual life. When they seem no longer capable of fulfilling their function for significant numbers of people, then revolution or reformist action to improve the situation also takes group form.[1]

As rabbis we are expected to foster religious experience and spiritual life among our people. The particular movement that claims us was, in part, a revolutionary response to the spiritual needs of ghetto-emancipated Jewry. Reform reasserted the centrality of the ethical *mitzvot* (according to prophetic Judaism), invalidated a substantial corpus of ritual requirements, and transformed the aesthetics of the worship service.

Liturgical Reform has always been at the core of our movement. Whereas in medieval times the rabbi rarely participated and never presided over a synagogue *minyan* (he worshiped with his disciples at home to save time for study), the Reform rabbi became the central officiant at public worship. Modern music, decorum, an abbreviated liturgy, prayers in the vernacular, the encouragement of attendance by women as well as men, and an inspirational sermon were all intended to enhance the spirituality of the service for an emancipated Western Jewry.

Spawned in Europe, these reforms found even more fertile soil on the American scene. Large, elegant sanctuaries reflected the expectation that worship would become the most popular form of public witness to the covenant and the major spiritual nurture for the Reform Jew.

How well did this liturgical reform succeed? The verdict is mixed. Many an American Jew did discover a greater comfort level and personal uplift in a synagogue where men and women worshiped together, dressed like their neighbors, and heard the familiar sounds of the vernacular. We all know a core of classical Reform Jews, weaned on the old *Union Prayerbook*, who maintain the discipline of regular worship and to whom the cadence of that liturgy is a warm balm.

But for many, indeed most, the discipline of regular worship became a non-*mitzvah*, and increasingly those who came in large

71

numbers to the synagogue were drawn more by the power of a charismatic preacher than the invitation to recite a reformed liturgy. Many of those preachers drew inspiration from the editorial pages of the newspaper and popular books rather than classic Jewish texts or overtly religious themes.

In time, even charismatic rabbinic sermons would not fill the cavernous sanctuaries. Only the High Holidays and Bar/Bat Mitzvah celebrations of large families with many friends would foster an aura of public witness to the Covenant. And those in the ranks with a professed need for spiritual nourishment would find the normative worship experience increasingly problematical. These seekers would stir our own uneasiness and lead to critical reflection on the need for a reform of Reform.

In 1920 Samuel Goldenson, a leading member of the Conference, addressed a CCAR convention on the theme "What Is the Real Influence of Judaism as a Religion upon the Jew of Today?" Goldenson acknowledged that "our question ... is itself a mark of the unsatisfactory state of our religious life." In tones reminiscent of the 1970s and 1980s discussion of Jews beguiled by the cults, Goldenson admonished his post-World War I colleagues:

> We must cease to indulge in futile polemics against and vain apologetics for the indifference of our people and for the tendency on the part of some to seek spiritual meat and drink elsewhere. We must acknowledge instead that such attitudes on their part issue not from caprice but rather from some genuine human want which we evidently do not satisfy. Instead of railing against them and calling their attention that we and our Bible have the material and inspiration given them by Christian Science, for example, we must bring the sustaining and life-giving nourishment to them directly with such zeal and enthusiasm, with such faith and consecration, that they will be drawn to us.[2]

Goldenson confronted his colleagues with the reminder that "we men engaging in labors that hold to unseen realities" should not expect easy evidence of success. But we cannot hope to succeed unless the rabbi is personally sustained by the faith he proclaims.

> It is not enough to call our people's attention to the fact that the Psalms are part of our own literature. ... The problem is for us to reaffirm their spiritual content not by word of mouth merely, but by example, an example that shall emanate from genuine feeling and a heartfelt appreciation of their pertinence and sublimity.[3]

Goldenson also suggested that the total burden of an inspiriting Judaism cannot be placed on public worship alone even in the

Reform synagogue. We need religious schoolteachers who "possess the love of their religion," lay leaders whose "spiritual character" is "an inspiring example," and "we must recover the spiritual atmosphere of the Jewish home by stressing more and more the need for personal and daily prayer."[4]

During the 1930s and early 1940s the interior life of the rabbi and his congregation received scant attention within the annals of the Conference. Many felt defensive about proclaiming "unseen realities" in the face of a scientific world view that rendered all unempirical assertions highly suspect and a psychoanalytic perspective that reduced religion to a neurotic crutch.

Many who entered the rabbinate during this period felt more summoned by the prophetic imperative of social justice than by any personal relation to the One in whose name the prophets spoke. Others saw themselves primarily as agents in the reconstruction of the social order and as defenders of the people Israel and its values. They felt more at home with the people and with humanity than with the One to whom Israel and humankind were bound in covenant. They felt more comfortable defending the people than the faith.

The Depression and the New Deal, the scourge of Fascism, the Holocaust, and the struggle for Israel's rebirth were their primary validating realities. Questions of spirituality and the quality of our inner life seemed irrelevant in a world that challenged our very right to live. Fighting anti-Semitism and promoting or opposing a national Jewish homeland kept the rabbinic adrenalin flowing. CCAR conferences, wrenched by debate on Zionism, had little energy or taste for an assessment of the Jewish life of the spirit.

In the aftermath of World War II reflection upon the monstrous evil of the Holocaust (which made simple humanism even more problematical than unqualified theism) and the heady days of Israel's rebirth engendered a new openness to the issues of the Jewish spirit within the Conference.

At the 1953 convention Jacob Weinstein heralded "the return to religion." He spoke as a Labor-Zionist and social activist whose earlier rabbinate had been more reticent in its theistic proclamations. Weinstein endorsed Chaim Greenberg's declaration that if you

abstract from the skein of our fate the strand of religious drama, especially in our long martyred exile, ... any attempt to interpret Jewish history becomes senseless. Jewish life over the past 2000 years was either a mystery (and a mystery has meaning and destination) or a misunderstanding. I assume that it was a mystery and I would be sorry for Zionism, for the whole idea of Jewish renaissance, if it could be regarded as the product of something incongruous, an historical faux pas.[5]

In that same address Weinstein made mention of the secular Yiddishists who were now sending their children to his Reform religious school. He anticipated the day when Labor-Zionist secularists would be able to feel at home in that synagogue. This endorsement of the "return to religion" portrayed a non-theistic humanism as patently inadequate for Jewish self-understanding or Jewish survival. An assertive *religious* liberalism was needed more than ever. In the aftermath of World War II most formerly anti-Zionist colleagues came to terms with Israel and many non-theistic colleagues reclaimed their religious birthright.

This is not to suggest that a confident theism has pervaded the Conference. In our time the *Lenn Report* (1967) found that only one in ten members of the CCAR believed in God "in the more or less traditional Jewish sense"; 62 percent believed in God "in terms of my own values of what God is and what He stands for"; 13 percent labeled themselves agnostics; one percent defined themselves as atheist.[6]

In his essay "The Training of American Rabbis," Charles Leibman noted that 67 percent of the student body at HUC-JIR believed in "a God to whom we can meaningfully pray." This decreased from 82 percent in the first year at HUC, and was further reduced to 50 percent in their last year.[7]

There is no reliable statistical survey on the faith quotients of earlier generations of rabbis. Undoubtedly, at least in the modern era, there have been colleagues who suffered the pangs of the priest Don Emanuel in Unamuno's story. The priest had lost his faith and so, as he raised the chalice of wine his hands trembled and cold sweat poured from him. Don Emanuel professed a faith he did not possess, but the people needed him to do what he did, so he lived a noble lie.

To be sure, the plight of a faith-shorn rabbi may be less traumatic. Judaism offers considerable theological leverage. We do not force congregants into theological corners, and we have come to expect the same immunity for ourselves. The very questions Lenn asked in his survey seem now strangely inappropriate. Our tradition of wrestling-struggling-doubting grants us kinship with Rabbi Levi Yitzhak of Berditchev whose challenges to the Almighty we delight to recount. Modern reformulations of Jewish theology have also helped preserve rabbinic integrity by offering options that appear to make less strenuous demands on our capacity for faith. And yet, the lack of a robust faith must still take its toll and limit our capacity to serve as spiritual mentors.

Spiritual Reawakening

This centenary period finds our movement challenged to be more assertive in its God-talk. The quest for the sacred has attained new respectability in our time. The larger cultural scene is more supportive of this quest. Sophisticated students of science, devoutly appreciative of its limits, now grant legitimacy and truth value to other modes of discourse. A new interest in religion has surfaced on the more academically prestigious campuses. In my student days, *agada* was the equivalent of nice stories to illustrate a point. Today cognitive psychologists such as Jerome Bruner speak of "the narrative mode" as an essential, irreducible vehicle for the experience and communication of life's transcendent meaning. The rise of religious fundamentalism with its challenge to the traditional view of a religiously neutral society and the movement toward theological deepening and more ritualized worship in the mainline liberal Christian churches have also had an impact.

Nor should we underestimate the effect of massive affluence. One must first be sated with bread before discovering that one does not live by bread alone. The increase in searchers and seekers within congregations is often most apparent among those who have leisure and the means to explore ways of deepening the quality of their lives.

All of this is still not to suggest a spiritual landslide. Our religious enthusiasm is conditioned by the milieu in which we were reared. God-talk does not come easily to our people's lips. We are a people who have developed, sometimes overdeveloped, our practical, critical minds. We are bright and clever and enterprising, and often caring and responsible, but too often we have been alienated from the deeper wellsprings of faith. Many closet believers have not permitted themselves to admit to others or even to themselves that there is a religious spark in their souls.

More than a few of us rabbis have also been closet believers. We have feared lest our image of sophistication and rationality be impaired by a public posture of piety. For years there was very little God-talk in our pulpits.

The climate is changing. An aggressive militant secularism is in retreat. Our preaching has been affected by the new *Zeitgeist*. Today the rabbi who speaks of personal faith will find a more responsive congregation. Only a few years ago, for the first time in CCAR history, the Conference sponsored a successful rabbinic *kallah* for spiritual renewal. Those in attendance delighted in receiving collegial support for personal religious statements. Today more colleagues draw unselfconsciously from the Jewish mystical tradition and invoke agada as the language of Jewish God-talk.

In its preliminary report to the UAHC Plenum, the Joint Task Force on Religious Commitment declared:

> Judaism is based upon an encounter with the one God. For too long we have been reticent to talk about our relationship with God. We need to cultivate within ourselves and in our children a greater sense of God's presence. Each of us must strive for a higher degree of spiritual sensitivity.[8]

Perhaps the greatest gift the CCAR can offer the movement in its effort at spiritual quickening is a text-literate rabbinate increasingly more comfortable with the role of spiritual guide. We are stewards of *agada*. To us is entrusted the master story that life is a covenant. That covenant may have hidden clauses, but beyond the mystery there is meaning.

Such affirmation did not come easily to our predecessors. We, too, are not spared periods of self-searing doubt and unrelieved anguish. But our influence must ultimately hinge on the power of personal witness. We model not only respect for *talmud Torah* and *menschlichkeit*, but also *emuna*, faith.

By its very nature, such faith remains more a struggle and yearning than a confident possession. There will be times when our vocational role impels us to proclaim more faith than we feel. Stationed on the battlefield as comforters of life's wounded, we may rise to spiritual affirmation we do not always feel in our souls. Are we then hypocrites? No, we are modeling that very amalgam of doubt and faith that is the price of living with a God who is both hidden and revealed. And yet, our own spiritual nurture and our power to nurture others is considerably enhanced if doubt and struggle are punctuated by moments when we, too, have experienced *gilui Shechina*, the nearness of the Holy One.

The role of defender of the faith is tempered not only by our personal religious struggle but also by the challenges of sophisticated congregants who eloquently present the evidence against a religious perspective. At such moments we may feel lonely and vulnerable. Even the naysayers, however, need our affirmation and want us to act as a barrier against which they may struggle. In us they find an echo of the other side of their hungering souls and on some level they want us to win the argument.

As guides of the Jewish spirit we walk a narrow ridge. Most of us are uncomfortable with the piety that presumes to be continually instructed by a *bat-kol*. We yearn for a middle ground that respects the rational structures of reality without denying our power to experience God's creative, guiding, and redeeming presence.

What is at stake in making Jewish spirituality a more respectable agenda? We cannot promise a higher Dun and Bradstreet rating or even greater peace of mind. We do offer the release from a certain shallowness. Those who ignore or suppress or deprecate religious questions are impoverished. Those intolerant of mystery, who glibly label themselves agnostics or atheists and then go on to other things — those who are not at least "atheists with an ache" — lack a dimension of inner depth.

It is a commendable rabbinic task to evoke our people's interest in what lies beyond the measurable. Our spiritual guidance should impel Jews to acknowledge the legitimacy of life's boundary questions: Why am I here? Why is there a right and a wrong? Why can I hope?

Revival of Ritual

In recent years the CCAR has sought to encourage more "religious observance." We have published a Shabbat manual, *Gates of Mitzvah, Gates of the Seasons,* and other guides. We would do well to examine how this trend relates to the quest for greater spirituality and religious commitment.

Many of our "classical Reform" elders perceived Judaism as a legacy of ideas rather than a discipline of ritual deeds. The ethical *mitzvot* were the primary way of acknowledging God's presence. Rituals were, at best, helpful ways of symbolizing our ideals and preserving the identity of the community. Rituals were a means of holding the vision in protective custody. The vision was primary. Ours was the task to proclaim publicly the message of "ethical monotheism." The Pittsburgh Platform put it thus:

> We hold that Judaism presents the highest conception of the God-idea as taught in our holy scriptures and developed and spiritualized by the Jewish teachers in accordance with the moral and philosophical progress of their respective ages. We maintain that Judaism preserved and defended ... this God-idea as the central religious truth for the human race.[9]

Over the years the Pittsburgh Platform legitimated a massive de-emphasis of ritual observance. In part, our elders were reacting against an encrusted Orthodoxy so preoccupied with ritual detail that the soaring vision of the faith was obscured.

By 1936, and the Columbus Platform, ritual observance received more favorable notice. "Judaism as a way of life ... requires the preservation of the Sabbath, festival and holy days

[and] the retention and development of such customs, symbols and ceremonies as possess inspirational value."[10] Even the declaration at Columbus fell short of suggesting a more direct link between ritual discipline and religious experience. Ritual was not viewed as a gateway to the sacred.

Anthropologist Clifford Geertz instructively affirms that

> whatever role divine intervention may or may not play in the creation of faith, ... it is primarily at least out of the context of concrete acts of religious observance that religious conviction emerges on the human plain.[11]

Yet, over the years we, too, have been prone to value ritual ceremonies only as ways of binding us to our people and symbolizing the values we cherish. We readily acknowledge that Judaism is a religion of deed rather than creed and cite approvingly the midrashic utterance attributed to God: "Would that they forsook Me and observed My commandments, for by so doing they will come to know Me." But we have not asserted explicitly enough the power of the ritual act to evoke and sustain a sense of our bond with the Eternal.[12]

The ritual of *Havdala* may have done more than we realize to resensitize our movement to the power of the symbolic act. Before the *Havdala* service regained its legitimacy as a Reform option in our congregations, it became popular in our youth camps. Classical Reform rabbis working with youth discovered that this brief, exotic, sensuous service released and channeled powerful sentiments in our young people. And our adult members, when exposed to *Havdala* at Board or family retreats, responded no less enthusiastically to its symbolism. We live in an age of proclamation by demonstration, an age of folk song and dance rather than formal oratory — an age to celebrate the mystery rather than demythologize it. We are now more inclined to teach our children how to live Jewishly than simply to talk about Judaism or Jewish values.

Reform's earlier deprecation of observance did not in itself yield a highly ethical or religious sensitivity. Doing less ritual *mitzvot* did not make us more religious. It must also be said that doing more ritual *mitzvot* will not necessarily yield a higher level of God-consciousness. Such discipline will be more spiritually effective for some than for others. There will continue to be those for whom the ethical deed will remain the most palpable symbolic way of responding to the Eternal Thou. But we are beginning to reassess the potential contribution of religious observance to spiritual deepening.

Spiritual Diversity

The recognition of diverse keys to the spiritual life should be kept in mind not only as we encourage more religious observance but also as we more vigorously assume the role of "defenders of the faith." In our teaching and preaching we are tempted to present most compellingly our own accommodation to the agadic framework. We respond to the problem of evil by asserting, as if it were Torah from Sinai, that God is radically self-limited and has no relation to pain and suffering. We may express utter disdain for the notion that, as Lord of Creation, God is somehow involved in the evil as well as the good, or that, in ways beyond our power to comprehend, God's purposes are being fulfilled even in those moments that bring us pain.

Over the years I have concluded that such a decisive doctrinal tilting in favor of a self-limited God constitutes unwarranted overreaching. I know persons who, in the midst of personal tragedy, have found more comfort from a God whom they believed to be in full control than a deity whose power has been neatly limited. I have also known persons whose faith required a radically limited God. And I have known those who shuttle between the two modes.

From classical rabbinic times the agadic legacy offered a variety of theological possibilities. There were rabbis who stressed Israel's suffering as punishment for sin ("Because of our sins were we exiled"), while others regarded human anguish as a setback for God as well as God's children. Of Israel's redemption from bondage, God says: "You and I went forth from Egypt" (Exodus Rabba 15:13). The contemporary rabbinic agadist would do well to proclaim a personal theological preference without denying congregants the comfort of an alternate vision or story.

What is true of theodicy is no less true of the broader quest for spirituality. Persons of different temperaments will need alternate ways to embrace the Holy One. Historically, Judaism has offered the religious seeker more than one path. Neal Gilman enumerates three Jewish modes of spirituality. There is the behavioral mode: "Through a conscientious life of mitzvah observance the Jews draw closer to the divine presence." And a pietistic mode:

What God wants most is inner devotion. That elusive term *kavanah* ... is eloquently expressed in the piyyut *yedid nefesh*: "Soul mate, loving God, compassion's gentle soul, take my disposition and shape it to your will."

This yearning for a sense of divine immediacy is embodied in the Jewish mystical tradition as well. Finally, the intellectual mode "claims that what God wants above all is knowledge, understanding, the mind. ... The study of Torah became the primary form of religious expression."[13]

By temperament the rabbi is drawn more to one model than another; so, too, are our congregants. True to ourselves we reveal a preference, and we model our rabbinate accordingly, but wisdom dictates that we not present our spiritual path as the only one. Some pietists among us will need an informal lay-centered worship alternative, while others will respond best to a Torah seminar. Both deserve our encouragement.

The Limitations of the Rabbinate

After we duly cultivate our own spiritual garden and provide our congregants with diverse paths of enrichment, we must still assess those structured occasions when the rabbi as spiritual guide interacts with fellow Jews. We turn first to the rabbi as presider at worship.

The Reform movement assigns the rabbi an unprecedentedly central role in the worship service. We who have functioned under this system must regard it as a mixed blessing. At times all the elements coalesce to provide an hour of radiant *kedusha*. The liturgy, the music, the tone set by our reading, and the congregation's response confirm the spiritual vitality of our movement. At other times the hour of worship is grievously flawed for us and, we suspect, for our people. What forces conspire to overwhelm our spiritual intentions?

As presider, the rabbi is in a precarious position. Too easily we can become preoccupied with the level of our performance and seek to evoke in others what we do not feel ourselves. Most precious are the moments when we are moved by setting and liturgy and radiate an inner plenitude or yearning. Such *kavana* cannot be programmed.

Another obstacle to worship is the discordant expectation of the worshipers among us. Many have come that particular Sabbath to witness a Bar/Bat Mitzvah of a relative or friend. We look out upon a congregation of restless captives. On those occasions when there are no "special events," the worship experience may be equally impaired by too many empty seats in a cavernous sanctuary. Worship requires the hint of a responsive community. A bare *minyan* will do in a tiny chapel; many more bodies are required for a credible *minyan* in a large sanctuary.

To this we must add problems in liturgical content and form. The new liturgy has its share of compelling rhetoric and poetic imagery, but the responsive reading, that major interplay between pulpit and pew, is often more a cognitive discourse than an invitation to affective response. Liturgy works best when it is spare, simple, and repetitive, or when the congregation responds to familiar melody. Generally, our congregants are exceedingly passive. To be sure, the cantor's solo and the choir's intricate arrangements may evoke a spiritual response, but such pulpit leadership needs to be balanced by the worshiper's power to feel personally invested as active partner.

While the list of obstacles could be multiplied, we have yet to penetrate the heart of the matter. At the 1969 CCAR convention, Morris Lieberman proffered the conclusion that

> in today's and tomorrow's thought world ... the way of prayer cannot meaningfully be followed. ... This would leave only the way of justice and righteousness, fulfilling remarkably the religious views of Amos. ... The line of spiritual evolution would thus lie from *amidah* as sacrifice to *avodah* as supplication, to *avodah* as social service, as the mode of relating us ... to the Infinite.[14]

Lieberman claimed that worship failed to appeal to the new religious mentality. "Supplication (and praise) of God are no longer meaningful to large masses of Jews." Tempting as this conclusion appears, I do not find it compelling. One would assume that most of those who absent themselves from worship no longer pray. Yet, in the private urgencies of their life, many seventh-day-absentists will utter a spontaneous petition. They dab a moist eye or exude a radiant glow as their child is blessed at Bar/Bat Mitzvah, and are moved to different tears by the *El Malei Rachamim* or the *Kaddish*.

Here is an important clue to the limitation of our normative worship experience. By its very nature, worship is intended to evoke the sense of community. The liturgy rehearses the people of Israel's life with God. Such worship functions best when the participants feel consensually bonded: board members at retreat, friends in a *chavura*. When those assembled feel a prior sense of community, public worship becomes the confirmation of that bond. At times of social and political dislocation (e.g., the aftermath of Martin Luther King's assassination or a destructive tornado), worship may evoke a sense of instant community. Persons are drawn to the sanctuary to huddle together, share their fears, and reaffirm their faith in the promise of the future.

But the need for community is counterbalanced by a more pervasive preoccupation with self. Generally, our worship does not address this need sufficiently. The liturgy calls us to indentify with God's liberation of Israel from Egypt while we are preoccupied with a personal bondage at home or in the marketplace. The prayers petition God for communal peace and redemption while we are assaulted by a soul-searing inner turmoil. People who avoid public worship have not necessarily outgrown the need for prayer, but they can pray in solitude, undiverted by other people or by a liturgical agenda that seems singularly inattentive to the ache in their souls. So, not surprisingly, the same individuals who find scant meaning in the discipline of public worship will be deeply affected by the blessing of their child in the synagogue or the child's Bar/Bat Mitzvah, or the recitation of the *Kaddish* at the funeral of a loved one. Any future liturgical efforts should seek to be even more evocative of these individual yearnings. Perhaps we should also reincorporate some of the *"davening* mode" (text-focused individual prayer), which more easily permits one to relate personally to God in the presence of the congregation.

Let us not, however, judge worship only by its power to address the me-centered self. Our task as spiritual guides is to foster the impulse to self-transcendence. There is nobility in evoking a concern for the welfare of those beyond our households and in regularly proclaiming public witness to the covenant and its teaching, and, however much we personalize the litrugy, the mass of our constituency will not be transformed into regular Temple-goers. Worship will remain an expression of spirituality for a limited, but, we hope, growing number of our people. As rabbis, we shall continue to feel specially bonded to those "regulars" in our ranks.

The Importance of Preaching

What of the preaching role? Recent generations of rabbis have devalued preaching. Fewer colleagues publish sermon topics, as if to concede that Jews are less likely to venture to the synagogue in pursuit of a particular message. The present generation of preachers finds it harder to prepare rigorously and mobilize its best energies for a role that seems to yield less ego-nourishing returns. Of course, the less rigorous preparation may activate a vicious cycle of less worthy sermons and even smaller attendance. Our age has also invested more creative energy in vitalizing worship and reducing the passive spectator mode of one-directional communication between pulpit and pew. We have downgraded the sermon's efficacy as energizer of the Jewish mind and soul.

Nevertheless, preaching remains an important arrow in our spiritual quiver. It can affect Jewish lives. Well-constructed, well-presented pulpit messages enable us to reaffirm the cogency of the heritage. At our best, we retell old stories with new names and places. (The Tower of Babel is alive and well in this generation's scramble for fame and fortune.) The creative connections we make between a Torah imperative (*halacha*) or a Torah narrative (*agada*) and the sensibilities of our people help bind them to the heritage and to us, their spiritual guides.

At times, events in the larger society cry out for public comment. There is a perceptible need for clarification, instruction, and closure. The anguish of Israel's Lebanon War in the summer of 1982 and a Wall Street scandal in which our co-religionists were conspicuous engendered a deep need for a rabbinic *devar Torah*. To miss the signal or falter in our response is to lose a teachable moment. The validation of our preaching efforts may come from congregants sometimes weeks or even months later when they declare, "You were speaking to me" (i.e., through you, Judaism spoke to me). Sometimes the fruit is even more tangible: a substantial contribution to the local hunger coalition in response to a sermon on the *mitzvah* of feeding the hungry.

When is preaching most effective? When what we offer is clearly differentiated from what may be received on television or the Op-Ed page of the *New York Times*; when what we say seems credibly derived from our serious encounter with the texts of Torah; when we preach to ourselves and risk sharing some of our own struggle for Jewish integrity; when we express respect for our people's dilemmas and the ambiguity of their lives; when our judgment is tempered by genuine love; when we are both intellectually respectable and unabashedly soulful.

Preaching is a difficult art which none fully masters. To take this form of teaching seriously is at times a humbling experience. We usually know when we have failed, but the moments of success are personally exhilarating and offer precious reminders of our spiritual influence. Many of us reach hundreds, some of us thousands, of Jews each month with a personal *midrash* on Torah. To devalue this opportunity is to deprive ourselves and our people.

The age of computers has not invalidated the face-to-face sharing of a message with the congregation of Israel. On the contrary, such sharing may be more important than ever. In his book *Megatrends*, John Naisbitt suggests that the proliferation of high-tech has engendered a greater need for "high-touch" experiences. Computer home-shopping will not replace visits to the shopping mall anymore than the video recorder will replace trips to the movies. At its best the synagogue worship experience, including an effective sermon, offers a precious affirmation of our bond to a community and confirms the strength that community's heritage bestows.

The Abiding Wisdom of Torah

Some who do not resonate to the cadence of communal worship or preaching will find a moment of *kedusha* in a guided and active encounter with sacred texts. Most often we ourselves "study in order to teach." While not technically *lishmah*, such study can be a form of personal renewal. I feel most authentic when my books are strewn across a large table and I am checking out a *midrash* to a particular Torah text. On many occasions the text will elicit a strained or even negative response. A Reform rabbi feels no impulse to apologize for, or embrace, all that has been bequeathed. Still we feel most renewed when the rejection of one text is premised on our embrace of another. We and our people are spiritually fortified more by our affirmations than our negations.

Helping other Jews to appreciate and appropriate the abiding wisdom of Torah remains our most self-validating task. Jacob Neusner has argued that the entire thrust of the

> exegetical process is to link upon a single plain of authority and reliability what a rabbi now says with what the written Torah says. ... Rabbinic tradition makes no systematic effort to distinguish the revelation transmitted to an ancient prophet from an exegesis or a Torah teaching of a contemporary sage.[15]

There are moments when thoughts leaping into my mind, thoughts filtered through the Torah text, the rabbinic commentaries, and my own sensibilities have the feel of God's revealing presence, of *Torah Shebe-al Peh*. Those are the most cherishable moments of study or teaching. We are neither prophets nor the daughters or sons of prophets, but we are rabbis and the daughters and sons of rabbis, and there are moments of *talmud Torah* that cast us as instruments of the One whose teaching is revealed to us and through us. Neusner asserts the full implications of an oral Torah: "In the rabbi the word of God was made flesh. And out of the union of man and Torah, producing the rabbi as Torah incarnate, was born Judaism, the faith of Torah; the ever-present revelation, the always open canon."[16]

The rabbi is quintessentially a spiritual guide when he or she leads a group in discovering the evocative power of sacred texts. Such a mingling of students' and teachers' comments, of traditional and personal *midrash*, of the Torah story and our own, such interplay of anguished negation and warm embrace is a soul-sustaining expression of our role as teachers of the spirit. So it has always been, so it will remain.

The Rabbi's Role as Counselor

What of our role as religious counselors? What of the normal fears and uncertainties of life? Being human we are bound to question the adequacy of our powers and the prospects of the future. Are we to reduce the problematic of living to an agenda for psychotherapy? Is there anything in my religion that can help me cope with those fears about myself and the world which go with the human territory? Is there anything within my heritage that offers me the precious gift of meaning?

As agadist I know three primary stories. God is our creator and creator of the world. God has given us a way to live, which, if we follow it, can bring meaning. God is a helping, redemptive presence in this world. The rabbinic counselor is a reteller of these stories.

There is an irreducible dignity rooted in our relationship to the One in whose image we are created. We are precious even when we fail. The God who creates us and who loves us has given us powers and tasks. We need to discover how to match our powers to our tasks and to do those tasks as a way of serving God in the world. We must be less obsessed with whether we will succeed or be rewarded and focus more on the doing of the task as our offering to that part of God's world entrusted to our care. The story of God as redeemer-helper is the root of our faith. If we do what we are called to do with all our might, our efforts will not be for nought. The redeeming God opens new possibilities. The One who summons us will establish the work of our hands.

Is this counsel, derived from the agadic framework of Judaism, any less valuable than the word of the psychotherapist? The one is not reducible to the other. Neurotic conflicts need the distinctive skills of a trained specialist, but the rabbi-agadist may help others derive from the primary stories of the faith what Paul Tillich called "the courage to be." This role is needlessly compromised by our acceptance of a psychological reductionism. Persons who come to us for help in our office or in the pews of our sanctuary do not need us to paraphrase the canons of Freud. They want us to assist them to discover the healing power of Torah. That healing power is most accessible when the words we speak bear the mark of personal struggle and conviction.

Bestowing the Blessings

And what of our power to bless? The Reform movement has denied Jews of priestly lineage the prerogative to bestow the traditional benedictions. We do not consider ourselves the priest's successors. If pressed, we crisply disavow any special praying power. Our words, we insist, carry no distinct weight with the Eternal. Younger colleagues seem even more anxious to disclaim any priestly prerogative. Unlike their rabbinic elders, they will not raise their hands when dismissing the congregation in prayer even if they use the traditional formula.

And yet we do offer those words (often with hand on shoulders or head of the recipient) as new babies, Benei Mitzvah, confirmands, and bride and groom stand before us. At times we intone prayers at a patient's bedside. Such words of prayer or blessing, spoken by us at particular moments, have a resonance which the layperson's words lack. That resonance cannot be adequately explained by Milton Steinberg's assertion that "in the end the rabbi differs from his Jewish fellows only in being more learned than they, or more expert in the tradition they all share."[17]

What is the distinctive value of our words of blessing? Each moment of the life cycle brings to awareness the sense of life's grace-filled and threatening quality. The miracle of birth assails even the blasé, avowedly nonreligious among us. At such moments we know that we are the recipients of marvelous gifts, but physician and family members who hover over the newly-born also know the future is uncertain. That realization inspired a rabbinic *midrash* comparing birth to a ship leaving port for a voyage of unknown promise and peril. Hence, at the naming of a child, gratitude needs to be expressed and anxiety must be overcome. The same may be said of Bar/Bat Mitzvah or wedding. All are turning points that evoke joy and anxiety. Religion provides the language to respond to joy with gratitude and to anxiety with hope. There is much to challenge such hope and there are moments when we can, at best, tremblingly profess it. This is especially true when we preside at a funeral in the aftermath of a tragic death. Yet here, too, the liturgy and the eulogy are needed to articulate the shared grief and to affirm faith in the abiding value of a particular life. Most Jews, however secularized they appear, need some relation to the religious symbols through which that faith is expressed.

By virtue of the covenant we have chosen to embody and teach, we are uniquely able to connect Jews to the symbols of their faith. For those who on some level hunger for the gift of meaning, we are special agents of a meaning-bearing covenant. Our word of blessing is special to them not because we have intrinsic influence with the Holy One, but because they know us to be formally committed to the transcendent hope they wish to embrace. Therefore we can mediate and release their openness to the realm of the sacred.

The blessing we can uniquely bestow need not be limited to a life-cycle event or to a hospital sickroom. We do have special power to intensify guilt or mediate the balm of self-acceptance. A couple came to counsel with me in anticipation of a forthcoming marriage. Each had been married before. Their "courtship" had taken place while the woman was still married. They deceived her family, and when the truth was exposed, caused grief and pain to spouse and children. They now wished to embark upon a new life. In my study they needed to express guilt for the way their relationship had been initiated. They assured me they had sought forgiveness from the injured parties and had worked to heal their relation to their children. They now wished to embark upon a new life of blessing. My speaking with them of Judaism's belief in divine forgiveness contingent upon acts of penitence and my subsequent presiding at their marriage (in which I made discreet reference to the errors of their past and their yearning to build a life worthy of blessing) offered them a spiritual gift no therapist or civil judge could bestow.

We do have the power to bless as did the rabbis before us. We may resist the role or unctuously and pietistically abuse it. Our capacity to fulfill it depends not only on the recitation of the right words but also on our understanding and acceptance of the priestly dimension in the rabbinate. By virtue of our vocational commitment we become special agents in binding our people to the One who endows life with the gift of meaning.

The Distinctive Role of the Rabbi within Jewish Life

Clifford Geertz reminds us that religion in its symbolic and institutional form is a human response to the problem of meaning.

> The problem of meaning in each of its intersecting aspects is a matter of affirming, or at least recognizing, the inescapability of ignorance, pain and injustice on the human plain while simultaneously denying that these irrationalities are characteristic of the world as a whole. And it is in terms of religious symbolism ... that both the affirmation and the denial are made.[18]

The rabbi-agadist mobilizes Jewish symbols and helps Jews struggle to embrace them. Much of the time our people's actual lives seem far removed from this realm of the sacred. They are coping on secular levels with the challenge of earning a living, healing the body, or promoting group survival. Because the everyday world of "common sense objects and practical acts" so dominates our people's consciousness and our own, we may feel lonely serving as guides to the sacred. There remain, however, teachable moments when our people are especially open to the realm of *kedusha* and welcome assistance in relating the everyday world to that deeper sphere in which we have our being.

Those moments most validate our calling. After all our protestations that Judaism is ethnic rather than narrowly religious and that we are teachers of Jewish values and promoters of the well-being of the Jewish people rather than priests, we must finally acknowledge the synagogue as that singular institution within Jewish life most committed to an unbroken covenant binding God, Torah, and Israel. The time is ripe more fully to embrace our distinctive role as spiritual guides within that covenant. Here we shall discover our greatest vulnerability and our deepest reward.

NOTES

1 "Transcendence in Contemporary Piety," *The Religious Situation*, D. R. Cutler, ed. (Boston: Beacon Press, 1969), p. 901.

2 *CCAR Yearbook*, 1920, p. 324.

3 *Ibid.*

4 *Ibid.*

5 Quoted in *CCAR Yearbook*, 1953, p. 300.

6 "Future of Reform Judaism," Theodore I. Lenn, 1972, pp. 28f.

7 *American Jewish Yearbook*, 1968, pp. 3 and 112.

8 Joint Task Force on Religious Commitment UAHC/CCAR, Interim Report, 1985, p. 46. The Task Force was dissolved in 1987.

9 Quoted in Gunther Plaut, *The Growth of Reform Judaism* (New York: UAHC, 1965), p. 33.

10 *Ibid.*, p. 99.

11 "Religion as a Cultural System," *The Religious Situation*, D. R. Cutler, ed. (Boston: Beacon Press, 1968), p. 669.

12 The essays on *mitzvah* included in *Gates of Mitzvah*, edited by Simeon Maslin (New York: CCAR, 1979), pp. 97-105, do strive, from various theological perspectives, to view the performance of ritual acts as an expression of our relation to the sacred.

13 N. Gilman, "Judaism and the Search for Spirituality," *Conservative Judaism*, Winter 1985-86, pp. 5-18.

14 *CCAR Yearbook*, 1969, p. 211.

15 *Midrash in Context* (Philadelphia: Fortress Press, 1983), p. 135.

16 *Ibid.*, p. 137.

17 *Basic Judaism* (New York: Harcourt, Brace and World, 1947), pp. 154-155.

18 "Religion as a Cultural System," p. 664.

UNITY WITHIN DIVERSITY

Charles A. Kroloff

In the *Centenary Perspective* approved by the Central Conference of American Rabbis in 1976, the autonomy of the individual was affirmed as a central principle of Reform Judaism. Diversity was portrayed as indigenous to our movement. The differences distinguishing us were described not only as "precious," but also as Judaism's "best hope" for confronting the future.[1]

At the same time, we are warned in the *Perspective* that our differences must not "obscure what binds us together." What does bind liberal rabbis together? To what extent are they united within the diversity that has characterized the CCAR from its inception in 1889?

The unifying elements referred to in the *Perspective* are described in general, non-authoritative terms. In the area of religious practice, for example, "Reform Jews are called upon to confront the claims of Jewish tradition, however differently perceived, and to exercise their individual autonomy, choosing and creating on the basis of commitment and knowledge." In our relationship to the State of Israel, we are portrayed as "privileged" and "enriched" and as the recipients of "unique opportunities for Jewish self-expression."

The *Perspective*'s language is largely suggestive and encouraging. Rarely is it commanding or compelling. In only two areas does the terminology approach an absolutist stance. Affirmation of God is deemed "essential" to Jewish survival, while study of Torah is a "religious imperative ... whose practice is our chief means to holiness." True to Judaism's historic lack of a faith-test, the *Perspective* implies that belief in the Divine is necessary for the Jewish people to survive *qua* people, but not necessarily for individual Jews to survive *qua* Jews. Study of Torah is perhaps the single component expressed in obligatory language.

How is it that autonomy has been elevated to such a principled position in contemporary Judaism? For 18 centuries after the destruction of the Second Temple, rabbinic legal authority exercised expansive influence. To be sure, geographical differences and traditional rivalries divided our co-religionists in their interpretations and practices. The same halacha was not embraced in every ghetto or *melah*. Nor was the RaMBaM the only sage greeted with opprobrium. Rabbinic authority was challenged by Karaitic fundamentalists, Sabbatean messianists, and Zionist socialists. Yet, most Jews embraced, at least in theory, the bibli-

cal admonishment, "According to the law which they shall teach
you, and according to the judgment which they shall tell you, you
shall do."[2] True, it was not always obvious who "they" were. But
even in those cases where rabbinic hegemony was not clearly
established, powerful centripetal forces were set into motion by
the socioeconomic powers of the community. The rabbi's authority derived from the consent of the community that elected him.

As the community changed, so did the authority which it invested in the rabbi. The Enlightenment introduced Western men and
women to a new way of looking at themselves, as autonomous,
self-directed individuals. Driven by their rational powers, they
came to recognize that they had the right, ability, and responsibility to look critically at institutions and traditions and to effect
those changes which seemed to them to be reasonable and necessary. Eventually, this process had an impact on the Jewish world
which found the enticements of individualism, opportunity, and
equality irresistible.

It was in this setting that the American liberal rabbinate of the
late 19th century sought to harmonize the autonomy of the new
frontier with the traditions and continuity of their Jewish past. As
Jews passed through the portals of New York Harbor, and especially as they moved south and west, they found it increasingly
difficult to adhere to Shabbat observance, *kashrut*, and the myriad
of rituals dictated by Halacha.

Against this background, Emil G. Hirsch of Chicago Sinai Congregation argued in 1885 at the Pittsburgh Rabbinical Conference
(a precursor of the CCAR) for endorsement of Sunday services,
not as a substitute for, but as an addition to Shabbat. Adolf Moses
of Louisville reasoned that on Shabbat most of his congregation
was engaged in earning a living and only "women, children and a
few old men" attended Friday night or Saturday morning services.[3] The community had been transformed.

Isaac M. Wise, the architect of American Reform Judaism and
the founder of the CCAR, declared that while he was not opposed
to the idea of a Sunday service "where it is a necessity," he concluded that he could not recommend it. He admonished his colleagues not to depart Pittsburgh "divided on any point." Hence, it
was resolved

> that there is nothing in the spirit of Judaism or its laws to prevent the intro-
> duction of Sunday services in localities where the necessity for such ser-
> vices appears, or is felt.[4]

Wise engaged in a balancing act. Paradoxically, he nurtured
unity among his colleagues by respecting their rabbinic autonomy

(especially in matters affecting their functioning in the congregational setting). At the same time, he avoided the extremes. Hence, while he would not recommend Sunday services, neither did he object to them. In balancing local necessity with historic precedent, he advanced 19th-century American Reform toward its twin goals of unity and autonomy.

Emancipation was irreversible. Saturday had become a workday for most American Jews. Sunday services — assimilationist though they appear from our perspective — were actually a creative adaptation to new circumstances, designed to bring into the synagogue on a weekly basis those Jews who might otherwise attend twice a year or perhaps leave the faith altogether. In that sense, these adjustments were not unlike rabbinic responses to the destruction of the Second Temple or to Jewish communal dispensations permitting Jews to do business with Christians in medieval Europe.

Rabbinic authorities had long felt empowered to suspend certain rabbinic injunctions when circumstances required it for Jewish survival. The RaMBaM affirmed:

> If the rabbinical authorities find it necessary to set aside temporarily mandatory or prohibitory commandments of the Torah in order to restore many to the faith or to save many Jews from stumbling in other matters, they have the right to act according to the needs of the hour.[5]

Wise expressed caution when requested to endorse radical change. On the question of whether circumcision shall be required for male proselytes, Wise announced that while he saw no need for *mila* since it was not required by the Torah, he nonetheless did require it on the principle of "*yachid verabim — halacha kerabim,*" when there is controversy over the law, it is resolved according to the majority. "I am not willing," he stated, "in so important and incisive a question, to be an innovator on my own authority."[6] (One year later, the CCAR resolved that it considered it lawful and proper for any officiating rabbi to accept into the covenant of Israel a proselyte who had not been circumcised. The vote was 25 to five, Wise voting with the majority.)[7]

The Conference was the vehicle by which the individual autonomy of the rabbis would achieve legitimacy. Radical change seemed necessary, even to Wise. But without unified action, individual autonomy threatened to become *hefkerut*, total license.

Even with the authority of unified action, there had to be limits to the extent to which autonomy might lead the movement. Taken to its outer extremes, autonomy threatened the very unity which Wise sought. In 1894 Wise acknowledged that the self-emancipation of his co-religionists had "led to a dissolution of all bonds of unity ... so that an academic interference on the part of the rabbi had become necessary... to save the kernel."[8]

Wise had insisted that the CCAR "has the power and duty of the Beth Din under the laws of Moses and the Rabbis." However, he articulated the purpose of the nascent CCAR as the quest for "unity of sentiment — not by dictation and enactments — but by a reasonable and free exchange of views." The CCAR was to function "not as a legislative, but as an advisory body; not to enact laws, but to expound them in harmony with the spirit and demands of the age."[9]

A century later Michael Meyer would call this process the "slippery slope of Enlightenment," whereby Jewish learning and practice would gradually contract until a minimalist position solidified.[10]

As agreement on ritual practices became less of a concern to the CCAR, ethics was becoming a more acceptable rallying point for the liberal rabbis and their co-religionists. In that arena they would invoke the mandate of the Kantian categorical imperative (so act that your conduct could become a universal model). Eugene Borowitz suggests that "liberal Judaism proclaimed that a properly autonomous self exists essentially in response to the commanding power of ethics" and that the "sovereign power of the ethical claim" is embraced by Hermann Cohen, Mordecai Kaplan, and even Martin Buber.[11]

Reform rabbis were frequently bound together more by their pursuit of *tikkun olam*, repairing the world, than by their chanting of *Kiddush*, more by acts that enriched the common weal than by traditions that linked them to their Jewish past.

Consider Stephen Wise's and Samuel Mayerberg's dramatic and effective attacks on corruption in New York's Tammany Hall and Kansas City's Pendergast machine, or Charles Mantinband's early and lonely advocacy of civil rights in Hattiesburg, Mississippi.

From the perspective of Reform theology, they were doing God's work. Social justice, interpreted by the prophetic tradition, seemed prescribed by God. If Borowitz was correct that we are not as morally competent as we thought we are, then Reform rabbis needed the unifying direction of colleagues who harnessed the moral passion of the prophets to the social problems of their age. As Roland Gittelsohn has observed, "it is one thing to let justice roll down as waters and righteousness as a mighty stream. It is quite another to build an irrigation system that works."[12]

Reform rabbis helped construct the irrigation system of justice by going to jail for the "crime" of desegregation in St. Augustine, Florida, by being beaten by racists in Mississippi while registering voters, by being bombed in Atlanta, by marching against the war in Vietnam, and by boycotting grapes harvested under unjust conditions and unfair labor practices. And they did it mostly in small groups of like-minded colleagues who coalesced around the prophetic mandates that goaded the CCAR. (The rabbis who joined Dr. Martin Luther King, Jr., in St. Augustine actually left the Conference while it was convened in Atlantic City in 1964 to express solidarity with the civil rights movement.)

The modern foundation for such bold deeds of justice was laid by Stephen S. Wise. He united the Reform rabbinate behind the principle of freedom of the pulpit in his historic 1905 letter to Temple Emanu-El of New York City: "The chief office of the minister ... is not to represent the views of the congregation, but to proclaim the truth as he sees it."[13] That classic statement became the basis for the now firmly accepted principle that every rabbi must be free to speak his or her conscience from the pulpit, without interference or restriction from any other authority. That principle has been tested again and again in the 85 years since Wise's letter and remains to this day a cornerstone of the Reform movement. Without the prestige and force of the CCAR behind it, it is unlikely that it would have survived the pressures to which rabbis and congregations are constantly exposed.

Today, congregational lay leaders are among the staunchest advocates of pulpit freedom, even though the founding principles of the Union of American Hebrew Congregations declared that there would be no "interfering in any manner whatsoever with the affairs and the management of any congregations."[14] In theory that left the congregations free to restrict freedom of the pulpit. However, just as rabbinic autonomy had limits, so congregational autonomy was circumscribed. Congregations relinquished their theoretical right to deny freedom of the pulpit and, as we shall see below, ceded privileges and accepted obligations for the sake of unity and fairness.

Eventually, ethics bound to Jewish theology but untethered to the Jewish people and their traditions proved inadequate to the task of building a 20th-century liberal Judaism that would retain and expand the base of its adherents.

Isaac M. Wise had described the CCAR's emerging purpose as

> consolidation, permanency, lawful and uniform progress. It can neither make nor undo the progress, but it can control it, that no sound organs be cut from the living body.[15]

Was Zionism such a "sound organ," or could it be wrenched from the body of the Jewish people without doing irreparable harm? In 1885, the 18 rabbis convened in Pittsburgh responded:

We consider ourselves no longer a nation, but a religious community, and
therefore expect neither a return to Palestine ... nor the restoration of any
of the laws concerning the Jewish state.[16]

Rebuilding Zion was excluded from the early goals of the American reformers whose focus in 1885 was on the opportunities that
their "new homeland" offered them and whose Zion now seemed
to rest between the shores of the Atlantic and Pacific oceans. In
their enthusiasm to affirm the value of the Diaspora and the power
of the American industrial machine, Zion's significance was
diminished.

By 1937, however, the Columbus Platform proclaimed that "all
Jewry" had nothing less than an "obligation" to aid in the rebuilding of Palestine and to make it "not only a haven of refuge for the
oppressed, but also a center of Jewish culture and spiritual life."[17]

In barely one-half century the stone which the builders rejected
had become the chief cornerstone. Zionism had become obligatory, at least in principle. History was proceeding in a calamitous
direction for Jews, and the CCAR not only made a dramatic shift
on Zionism but also moved toward declaring anti-Zionists as
beyond the outer limits of Reform Judaism. Once again, the
CCAR called upon its members to relinquish a measure of autonomy (a) for the sake of Jewish survival, (b) to keep Reform
Judaism responsive to historic developments, and (c) to ensure
that Reform Jews would not distance themselves from the mainstream of the Jewish community.

The American Council for Judaism was founded by some members of the CCAR for the purpose of opposing Zionism. Following vigorous debate in 1943, in the shadow of the Holocaust, the
CCAR approved a resolution declaring that the ACJ "endangered
the unity of the Conference" and that "its continued existence
would become a growing threat to our fellowship." While not
restricting any colleague from expressing his convictions within or
without the Conference, the CCAR "urged" its members to
"terminate" the ACJ.[18] This was a frontal attack on unbridled
autonomy.

Samuel H. Goldenson accused the CCAR of denying its members the right of assembly guaranteed in the Bill of Rights. It was
later reported that "there was fear that this [action] would split the
Conference."[19] No schism ensued. Colleagues recognized that
rabbinic autonomy was not an absolute, just as the American
democratic process proscribes certain individual privileges for the
sake of the common weal. Taxation, fire regulations, and envi-
ronmental laws are among the limitations that give shape and
direction to our society.

The CCAR had emphatically proclaimed Zionism was a sound organ, to use Wise's phrase, and that it had a responsibility to its members, to Reform Judaism, and to *kelal Yisrael* to control the progress of Reform by ensuring that Zionism not be cut off from the living body. No prohibitions or penalties were invoked to achieve this end. The tone of the resolution was advisory, but it bordered on the authoritative. In response to Nazism and to the growing settlement of Palestine, the Conference determined that a measure of the individual rabbi's autonomy must once again give way to the obligations that history had presented.

Although its members have differed widely since 1943 in their interpretation of Zionism, the CCAR has reaffirmed again and again the obligation of all Jews to support the Jewish State. In addition to its unyielding commitment to Israel's military, political, and social strength, the CCAR has unanimously demonstrated its support for religious pluralism and full rights for progressive Judaism in the Jewish State.

As with the debate on Zionism in 1943, a sense of foreboding hung over the Conference in 1973 as its members gathered in Atlanta to debate a resolution on officiation at mixed marriages. The chair of the *Ad Hoc* Committee on Mixed Marriage, Herman Schaalman, observed that the 1909 declaration "discouraging" mixed marriage was sufficiently vague as "to provide option and *hechsher* for diametrically opposite views and practices." The committee therefore moved that the CCAR "now declares its *opposition* (emphasis mine) to participation by its members in any ceremony which solemnizes a mixed marriage."[20]

Once again, no prohibitions or sanctions were proposed. After free and open debate, the stronger standard was affirmed. True to the Conference's tradition of affirming the right of rabbis to dissent from positions taken, the resolution recognized "that historically its members held and continue to hold divergent interpretations of Jewish tradition."[21]

Although the operative paragraph, declaring opposition to officiation, passed by a three-to-two margin, there were few, if any, defections. While a substantial minority had dissented for varying reasons, few members publicly questioned the CCAR's *right* to take that position. Although differences of opinion endure years later, colleagues of diverse persuasions continue to function effectively within a Conference that has strengthened its standard against officiation at mixed marriages. The predicted doom did not materialize, demonstrating that the CCAR still had the capacity to "oppose" the practices of a significant minority without rupturing the Conference's unity.

From I. M. Wise to present day, history has demonstrated that rabbis require a Conference where colleagues and their teachers can examine both sides of an issue in light of Jewish learning and contemporary needs. Sometimes the available options are in direct conflict. Jack Stern described his perception of the CCAR's role at such junctures:

> I need my colleagues with whom I can discuss and debate and vote — and then return to my congregation and say, "This is the majority view with which I concur for the following reasons..." Or, on another occasion, I shall say to my congregation, "I dissent from the majority view...." And I would remind my congregation ... that Jewish tradition guarantees the right of dissent; that the Talmud itself, by recording the arguments of the dissenting minority, was in some measure according recognition to that very minority view.[22]

The CCAR has continued, and in all likelihood will continue, to set outer boundaries for Reform Jewish life and for rabbinic behavior. Beyond those boundaries are options which the Reform rabbinate has determined are "contrary to the interests of Jewish survival and Jewish tradition," to use Stern's words. Rabbis have been free to traverse those limits and, in so doing, have rarely been expelled from, or censured by, the CCAR. However, they did, on occasion, evoke the formal opposition of their colleagues when they moved beyond the limits which the majority of Conference members could tolerate in areas such as Zionism and mixed marriage officiation.

In the rabbi's professional life, there are also boundaries beyond which CCAR members have agreed not to trespass. In so doing, they have ceded some of their autonomy to groups of colleagues and laypersons who oversee certain professional standards and procedures. In setting limits in these areas, Reform rabbis properly focused on their personal responsibility and their own professional conduct.

As early as 1899, I. M. Wise proposed that the CCAR ensure the right of rabbis to be respected by every congregation and agree upon an ethical standard for rabbinic placement.[23] It took 56 years, but in 1955 the Reform rabbinate did impose upon itself a mandatory system of rabbinic placement in partnership with the UAHC and the Hebrew Union College-Jewish Institute of Religion. The CCAR approved the placement program so that fairness and equity might infuse that process. Although repeatedly challenged and modified, the placement program remains firmly in place as an expression of the rabbinate's commitment to equity within the profession.

With the ordination of women and their admission into the CCAR, the mandate of the Rabbinical Placement Commission was broadened to include the principle of non-discrimination in gender. Today that principle pervades the deliberations and functions of the CCAR and is a *sine qua non* for all leaders in the Reform movement. All CCAR publications since the late 1970s are gender inclusive. Once again, Reform Jews have relinquished some autonomy (the freedom to engage in gender discrimination) because reason and the community require it.

Through the National Commission on Rabbinic-Congregational Relations, the CCAR has joined with the UAHC in establishing standards for the rabbi's dignified retirement, orderly rabbinic transitions, contracts, benefits, staff relationships, and a host of other congregational-rabbinic concerns. Failure to adhere to some of the standards has resulted in sanctions against the offending party.

A Committee on Ethics and Appeals, consisting of some of the CCAR's most respected members, deals with issues arising from personal and professional conduct. The committee considers matters of commercialism, relationship between rabbis of different congregations and between rabbis of the same congregations, and other matters. In cases of violation of the Conference Code of Ethics, Placement Guidelines, other regulatory guidelines adopted by the CCAR, or misconduct rendering the rabbi unworthy of membership, the committee, after investigation, may exercise disciplinary action, including censure. The committee may also recommend suspension or expulsion to the Executive Board of the CCAR.[24]

In recent years, there has been a perceived need for further guidance to ensure that rabbis will conduct their personal and professional lives in consonance with the highest Jewish values. The draft version of the Code currently under consideration exhorts Reform rabbis to be "in control" of their own sexual lives, to act with "business and fiscal responsibility" in their personal lives, and to maintain relations with one another that are "above reproach."[25]

In point of fact, rabbis are rarely reprimanded, censured, or suspended for actions that the Code deems "unacceptable." Terms such as *prohibited* or *in violation of* are not used. One is struck by the leniency of the CCAR Code of Ethics when compared to those of other professional organizations. This seems to reflect an unwillingness to declare certain behavior not only unacceptable, but also beyond the limits that the Conference can tolerate. Currently the CCAR is considering adopting a clearer definition of

what those limits are and what sanctions might be imposed on
members exceeding those limits.

In the realm of Jewish ritual practice, we have in the past half
century increasingly heard calls for guidelines and codes. In his
Presidential Message of 1937, Felix Levy reminded his colleagues
that "discipline is at the core of the Decalogue." He therefore recommended "a code of rules for guidance in practice." Not intended to be "final or even obligatory," it would rather serve as "guide
and thereby approximate to a uniformity of ritual so badly
needed."[26]

Levy anticipated the growing interest in standards that would
become manifest three and four decades later. By the 1970s,
Reform rabbis were persistently being asked: What is it in Jewish
tradition that is non-negotiable for the liberal Jew? Besides the
imperative of Torah study and the freedom to choose from
options, what else do you stand for? Can a Reform rabbi do anything and still remain a member in good standing of the CCAR?

Reform Jews have discovered that, as their faith evolves, they
experience a growing need for rubrics, structure and definition.
Hefkerut leaves them floundering in a sea of choices. Radical
freedom, torn away from discipline and structure, often results in
"every Jew doing what is right in his or her eyes."

During a visit to the fitness center of our local "Y," I encoun-
tered a man whose father had died two days earlier. With a look
of embarrassment, he asked, "Rabbi, is it alright for a Reform
Jew to 'work out' during *Shiva*?" Among the responses available
to me as a Reform rabbi were the following: (1) the CCAR's
guide, *Gates of Mitzvah*, "encourages" you to be at home for at
least three days;[27] (2) if exercise is essential to your health, you
are permitted to do so on the basis of *pikuach nefesh*, saving a
life; (3) as a liberal Jew you have a number of options, including
the halachic prescription of seven days. It is up to you to make an
informed choice.

The question persists: How much tradition is negotiable? In my
weakest moments, I fear, along with many colleagues, that if I
speak of obligation or requirement, if I insist too hard that minimal is not enough, some members will return to the anonymous
host of the unaffiliated. But on reflection I realize that the opposite is the case. Reform Jews today want more, not less, guidance
for themselves and their children, especially in response to the
hefkerut that pervades the secular society.

Jacob Rudin was right: "such authority as the Reform rabbi pos-
sesses derives not from his scholarly competence," but from the
characteristics of his personality.[28] Our emphasis and that of our
congregants on the rabbi as "personality" rather than as interpreter

of an evolving tradition reinforces the trend toward radical autonomy at the expense of communal discipline.

There is a basis for standards reinforced by communal discipline in the Reform rabbinate. Historically, the CCAR has provided its members with well considered, authoritative positions on matters of social justice, Israel, Jewish education, personal status, and Reform Jewish practice. Time and again those positions have reinforced my efforts to respond to the needs of my congregants. Instead of stating, "Rabbi Kroloff recommends...," I have been able to assert, "the CCAR has affirmed ... and Rabbi Kroloff endorses...."

This affirmation of standards need not be divisive. Indeed, it can be unifying, especially if developed in the spirit proposed by Jack Stern, by "a community of Reform Jews with such built-in mutual respect that the majority on any given issue will avoid the pitfall of *azut panim*, of tyranny and arrogance, and that the minority will avoid the pitfall of *hitpardut*, of separation and schism."[29]

The CCAR Committee on Responsa receives more than 100 inquiries annually. This demonstrates that Reform rabbis recognize the persuasive nature of these responsa. While they are not imposed as authoritative, they represent a communal standard for the movement.

The guides published privately and by the CCAR with the approval of its membership represent a growing recognition of the dangers of *hefkerut* and the need for a code of Jewish conduct. When David Polish and Frederic Doppelt published *A Guide for Reform Jews*, they were motivated by the belief that freedom means "not to turn order into chaos, but rather to go from one form of order to another form of order."[30] Polish and Doppelt never suggested that the CCAR publish their *Guide* because they were convinced that such a proposal would have evoked bitter controversy. Since then, the CCAR has published *A Shabbat Manual*,[31] *Gates of Mitzvah*,[32] *Gates of the Seasons*,[33] and *Gates of the House*,[34] none of which undermined the individual freedom of Reform Jews.

The CCAR has become for some of its members a *chevra*, a rather closely knit community of colleagues who turn to one another for intellectual, emotional, and spiritual support. From time to time small groups of concerned colleagues have coalesced into *chavura*-type gatherings, not unlike those initiated by Harold Schulweis in his Encino, California, synagogue in the 1960s. He was responding to the felt need of his members for support in their pursuit of Jewish social, religious, intellectual, and family interests. (That experiment yielded more than 60 *chavurot* in Schulweis's congregation alone and thousands in synagogues across the continent.)

Reform rabbis seek reinforcement and standards for their personal religious lives as well as for their guidance to congregants. Some are willing to relinquish a measure of personal autonomy in order to strengthen those standards. No less than four recent CCAR presidents have proposed that colleagues who share a vision of higher standards create rabbinic support groups for purposes of study and exploration.

Some Reform rabbis were disappointed when *Divrei Gerut* (Guidelines Concerning Proselytism) offered only "guidelines and suggested procedures" intended as "a working consensus of practice within the Reform rabbinate, rather than a set of standardized requirements."[35] Eugene Lipman recently suggested that colleagues specifically interested in exploring conversion standards should convene for purposes of study.[36]

As in all movements of Judaism, there are groups of rabbis who strive to maintain the highest possible standards for conversion. They need the insights that flow from collegial interaction and the reinforcement that emerges from mutually agreed upon criteria. Our community has also changed. More than ever, Reform Jews-by-Choice care whether their conversions meet standards set by our movement and are recognized by all Reform and Conservative rabbis.

From a process of study, conversion standards might emerge which the participating rabbis could voluntarily accept as authoritative for themselves. Such a group might evolve into a regional or national *chevra* of Reform rabbis who accept a self-imposed discipline for conversion. A model for this exists among Reform rabbis in Toronto.

The Reform rabbinate, with its rich diversity, would benefit from the proliferation of small groups encouraged by the CCAR. Some might be mandated by the Conference membership; others might be voluntary associations of colleagues. Each would adopt an area to study, explore, and invite reactions. Subjects for exploration might include Shabbat, *gerut*, divorce and other matters of personal status, spirituality, the rabbi's religious life, continuing education, *kelal Yisrael*, and other issues on which unified rabbinic positions with peer support could be helpful in establishing standards. Some of these groups might eventually seek the support of colleagues throughout the Conference; others might function at a local or regional level.

There is risk inherent in such exploration which we must acknowledge. Forces could arise that might seek to impose a "Reform orthodoxy" upon our movement or encourage schisms in our movement. Such an eventuality is possible but unlikely, because the CCAR has already withstood the test of passionate dissent and indeed transformed it into a healthy process of discovery.

On the other hand, the *status quo* is fraught with greater danger. We are on the verge of becoming "all things to all Jews." As ethics untethered to the Jewish people proved inadequate to the task one-half century ago, so today our lack of clear expectations and criteria for ourselves and our congregants renders us ill-prepared to meet the needs of Jews who seek our guidance and direction as they return to Jewish life.

Rabbis themselves face a special challenge in their personal religious lives. Consider Shabbat. We teach it. We preach it. But, as Samuel Karff asks: "Do we live what we sell?" We urge others to cease work on Shabbat, yet we "work" the hardest on the day of rest. We take the Shabbat table seriously, yet we probably rise up from it faster than any other religious Jew in order to fulfill our synagogue duties. CCAR members have grappled with these issues in seminars and informal settings and have arrived at ways of reconciling the personal and the professional without impairing either. They have been united in their search for solutions. Without such a unified quest, the rabbinate would often be too lonely to endure.

Rabbis also turn to each other for help in dealing with issues of faith. In 1980, the CCAR brought 50 rabbis together at the Monhonk (New York) Conference Center to explore issues of spirituality in the rabbinate. The Monhonk discussions gave rise to similar gatherings throughout the country. As colleagues shared, they recognized that they were united in their quest for a more spiritual dimension to life and in their commitment to help all Jews experience that faith. Nearly all Reform rabbis affirm the power of God in human life. They seek to understand what it is that God requires of them and to live by those expectations which most term *mitzvot*.

In our zeal to protect rabbinic autonomy, we have too often permitted ourselves to travel in so many diverse directions that our effectiveness as Reform Jews has been crippled. We need to take risks to become demanding of ourselves. On occasion that process has found expression in small, informal groupings, often initiated by the CCAR. During the past hundred years, the Conference itself has been the vehicle by which rabbis have affirmed, by majority vote, often overwhelmingly, many positions and principles around which they could unite for greater impact on our movement and the Jewish and secular communities. These have included respect for local necessity within the context of historic precedent; social justice; freedom of the pulpit; the security, democratic character, and religious pluralism of the State of Israel; opposition to officiation at mixed marriage; personal and professional ethics; orderly placement procedures; gender equality; study of Torah; codes of Jewish practice, and the quest for the spiritual.

In the next 100 years, the CCAR will continue to respect and encourage diversity. But there will be limits beyond which toleration may not be possible, and there must be an evolving standard for Reform Jews from which we can sense that we have been commanded to fulfill *mitzvot*.

NOTES

[1] *CCAR Yearbook*, 1976, pp. 174-178.

[2] Deuteronomy 17:11.

[3] Walter Jacob, ed., *The Pittsburgh Platform in Retrospect* (Pittsburgh: Rodef Shalom Congregation, 1985), pp. 115-119.

[4] *Ibid.*, p. 119. The felt need for unity is perceived in the reaction of Joseph Krauskopf of Kansas City: "I have been laboring to improve the attendance [on Shabbat] ... yet if the Conference will state that there is no objection to Sunday services *where there is a necessity* (emphasis mine), I will not raise a dissenting voice."

[5] Hilchot Mamrim II, 4, see Samuel S. Cohon, *Essays in Jewish Theology*, "Authority in Judaism," (Cincinnati: Hebrew Union College Press, 1986), p. 70.

[6] *CCAR Yearbook*, 1891, pp. 85-86.

[7] *CCAR Yearbook*, 1892, p. 36.

[8] *CCAR Yearbook*, 1894, pp. 72-73.

[9] *CCAR Yearbook*, 1893, p. 9.

[10] "The Impact of Enlightenment and Anti-Semitism on Modern Jewish Identity," Lecture, CCAR Convention, Cincinnati, Ohio, June 23, 1989.

[11] "Autonomous Jewish Self," *Modern Judaism*, vol. 4, no. 1, February 1984, p. 41.

[12] "Judaism and Social Justice," Lecture, Rockdale Temple, Cincinnati, Ohio, November 15, 1955.

[13] Stephen S. Wise, *Challenging Years* (New York: Putnam, 1949), p. 91.

[14] *Proceedings of the first General Convention and Preamble, Constitution and By-Laws*, UAHC, July 8-10, 1873, vol. 1, pp. 7-9.

[15] *CCAR Yearbook*, 1894, p. 67.

[16] *The Pittsburgh Platform in Retrospect*, p. 108.

[17] *CCAR Yearbook*, 1937, pp. 94-114.

[18] *CCAR Yearbook*, 1943, p. 93-95.

[19] *CCAR Yearbook*, 1973, p. 96.

[20] *Ibid.*, pp. 59-63.

[21] *Ibid.*, p. 97.

22 *CCAR Yearbook*, 1975, p. 188.
23 *CCAR Yearbook*, 1899, p. 29.
24 *Code of Ethics,* New York, CCAR, adopted 1982.
25 *Code of Ethics* (draft version), New York, CCAR, May 1988.
26 *CCAR Yearbook*, 1937, p. 183.
27 New York, CCAR, 1979, p. 59.
28 *CCAR Journal*, October 1962, pp. 8-9.
29 *CCAR Yearbook*, 1975, pp. 189-190.
30 New York, Ktav, 1973, p. 9.
31 New York, Ktav and CCAR, 1972.
32 New York, CCAR, 1979.
33 New York, CCAR, 1983.
34 New York, CCAR, 1977.
35 *Divrei Gerut* (New York: CCAR, 1983), p. 1.
36 Presidential Address, CCAR, Cincinnati, June 23, 1989. p. 1.

ISRAEL AND THE REFORM RABBINATE*

Marc Saperstein

The history of the Reform movement's attitudes toward Zionism, including the dynamics of its repudiation of an early principled anti-Zionist stance, has been masterfully told in studies by David Polish and Howard Greenstein,[1] and there is no need for recapitulation. Instead, I shall attempt to address some of the theoretical problems relating to the Land and State of Israel that face the movement today, and to outline options that emerge from the history of Reform and from the tradition of classical Jewish literature and thought.

A convenient framework is the Jerusalem Program of the World Zionist Organization, ratified by the 27th Zionist Congress in 1968. This ideological base, formally adopted by ARZA but not by the CCAR or UAHC as a whole, affirms that the aims of Zionism are:

1. The unity of the Jewish people and the centrality of Israel in Jewish life.
2. The ingathering of the Jewish people in its historic homeland *Eretz Yisrael* through *aliya* from all countries.
3. The strengthening of the State of Israel which is founded on the prophetic ideals of justice and peace.
4. The preservation of the identity of the Jewish people through the fostering of Jewish and Hebrew education and of Jewish spiritual and cultural values.
5. The protection of Jewish rights everywhere.

It is difficult to imagine serious controversy within the Reform movement about the fourth and fifth points. But the first three raise issues of interest and concern that deserve to be articulated and explored.

The Centrality of Israel in Jewish Life

Like the "unity of the Jewish people," an axiom frequently invoked without full clarity about its meaning, the "centrality of Israel" raises some challenging questions of historical importance and contemporary urgency. The theoretical goal is to find an appropriate model for a proper and healthy relationship between the Jewish communities of the Diaspora and the *Yishuv*. But something more is at stake, a problem that cuts to the heart of Zionist thought: the legitimacy, authenticity, and validity of continued Jewish life in the Diaspora at a time when settlement in the

Land of Israel is both a realistic choice and, according to many, a vital need. In order to address this issue, we will need to outline the ideological options and their roots in traditional Jewish thought.

One extreme model is implied by the phrase "Negation of the Diaspora." As Ahad Ha'am noted,[2] this phrase is itself ambiguous, and can be understood both in an objective and a subjective sense. Objective negation insists that it is impossible for Jewish life to be sustained in the Diaspora once social isolation and the governmental sanction of Jewish communal authority is ended. In recent years, this argument has generally taken a demographic form, relying on statistics about low Jewish birthrates, high rates of intermarriage, powerful pressures to assimilate, and minimal levels of Jewish education and observance. The conclusion is that Jewish life outside the Land is doomed, and that all who are committed to Jewish survival must bind up their destiny with the *Yishuv*.

Subjective negation of the Diaspora entails a value judgment. No matter what the demographic figures might indicate, there is something inherently illegitimate about Jewish life "in exile." As one of the extreme Zionist negators put it, "The Judaism of the Galut is not worthy of survival."[3] The rhetorical question of the Babylonian exiles — "How can we sing God's song in a foreign land?" (Ps. 137:4) — encapsulates this position, implying that authentic Judaism in the Diaspora is at best problematic and may well be a contradiction in terms. Though never unanimously accepted, traces of this view can be detected throughout traditional literature.

The opposite extreme places the Diaspora on a higher religious level than the Land of Israel as a setting for Jewish life. Such a position is frequently associated with the ideology of the Reform movement, but evidence of its existence can be found in virtually every age of Jewish history. Admittedly, it is more difficult to identify coherent statements of this position before the 19th century; the ideology of Diaspora living must often be reconstructed from the arguments of its opponents. But the very fact that Jews felt impelled to repudiate such thinking bears witness to its tenacity and appeal. Though rarely a central article of faith, the view that Diaspora life was not only legitimate but in some sense crucial to the fulfillment of the Jewish vocation was by no means as unusual as is often claimed.

The clash of extreme alternatives is encapsulated in a celebrated exchange between two of the intellectual giants of modern German Jewry, Hermann Cohen and Martin Buber. As Buber put it,

"The entire history of Judaism," says Cohen, "teaches, in accordance with the vision of the prophets, that the realization of Judaism is grounded in our dispersion among the peoples of the earth." We have learned the opposite lesson from history, namely, that in a life of dispersion not determined by ourselves, we cannot realize Judaism. We can pray here in the Diaspora, but not act; bear witness to God with patience, but not with creativity; praise the jubilee year, but not usher it in.[4]

Neither the position that denies any legitimacy to Jewish life in exile nor the position that asserts the clear superiority of the Diaspora to the *Yishuv* is likely to have much resonance in Reform thinking today. Any view that would deny the possibility of authentic Jewish life in the Diaspora is too alien to the *Sitz-im-Leben* of Reform, and any fundamental denigration of the significance of Israel, whether through a repudiation of peoplehood or a glorification of powerlessness, seems too remote from the events of recent history, to win widespread support. But the legacy of these extreme stances, suitably modified, is still detectable in two intermediate positions that do present live options. Both affirm the legitimacy and authenticity of the Diaspora and Israel, but one insists that Israel is "central" to contemporary Jewish life with the Diaspora remaining on the periphery, while the second affirms a partnership of equality and mutual benefit.

Historically, this choice is reflected in the controversy between Ahad Ha'am and Simon Dubnow. In a well-known essay, Ahad Ha'am attacked the "Diaspora Nationalism" of Dubnow. Conceding that the Diaspora will not disappear and agreeing that Jewish national life in the Diaspora must be strengthened, he nevertheless denied that any Diaspora Jewish community could create a cultural life rich and vital enough to encompass the full legacy of Jewish spiritual values and creative energy. Such communities can at best be "nothing more than a sort of formless raw material until they are provided with a single permanent center, which can exert a 'pull' on all of them, and so transform the scattered atoms into a single entity with a definite and self-subsistent character of its own."[5] What the "spiritual center" had to offer the Diaspora is obvious; it is not clear what Ahad Ha'am believed the Diaspora could offer to the *Yishuv*.

Dubnow, responding, concurred that living in "Exile" is not a blessing, that full national-cultural life in the Diaspora is impossible, that "if we had the power to transfer the entire Diaspora to a Jewish state we would do it with the greatest joy."[6] Nevertheless, he insisted that the spiritual center in the Land of Israel cannot provide the entire Diaspora with "all the national energies necessary for revitalizing the Diaspora and securing its autonomous organization."[7] Influenced by the center in the Land, the Diaspora must mobilize its own energies for its own struggle. "The reciprocal influence of the two centers will create the mean for the national development of Judaism."[8]

Echoes of this debate still reverberate. Ahad Ha'am's model of centrality is reiterated in categories bearing distinctly theological overtones by the Zionist writer Harold Fisch, who seems to bear no hostility toward Diaspora Jewry and assumes that substantial Jewish communities will continue to exist outside of Israel, but who can find no real significance in their efforts as Jews. With the establishment of the State, and especially after the Yom Kippur War of 1973,

> the whole burden and charge of the Covenant had now passed to the people and state of Israel. What had occurred was a kind of changing of the guard. The Jews of the Diaspora would participate by proxy in the joys and trials of the Covenant, but the covenantal centre of gravity itself had passed to Israel. ... Jewish history was to move into a new channel; those who wished to participate in it would have to become part of the new enterprise in the land of Israel. ... The Jews of the Diaspora are in the position of having carried the burden to this point; and it is with an unconscious sigh of relief that they have discharged it and placed it on younger shoulders.[9]

This extraordinary paragraph, so reminiscent of Christian replacement theology, does not suggest that Diaspora Jewish life is neurotic or doomed. It is perfectly natural to want to hand over a burden to those with "younger shoulders." To live as a Jew in the Diaspora is simply, in this view, to say one's lines offstage, to avoid God's spotlight, to keep a safe distance from where the action is.

On the other hand, a position akin to Dubnow's has been vigorously argued by the important yet relatively neglected scholar and thinker Simon Rawidowicz. Raised in a Zionist family, passionately committed to Hebrew language and culture, Rawidowicz nevertheless energetically opposed the "Negation of the Diaspora" that imbued so much of Zionist thought, warning that it leads "to hatred not of exile alone, but also ... of Israel which is within it."[10] He also warned against a Diaspora content with a vicarious Jewishness, "satisfied with what takes place in Medinat Yisrael and [ignoring] the urgent needs of Bet Yisrael in the field of our communal and spiritual life."[11] Arguing from history, he laid the intellectual foundations for a symbiotic relationship of mutual enrichment:

It is the Diaspora which learns Torah and teaches it to Zion, which sends to Jerusalem sages and scribes, idlers and men of piety, who cause the crown of Torah to return to its splendor, whenever it is forgotten within Jerusalem from generation to generation, from Ezra to Rabbi Hiyya and after him, to the twentieth century.[12]

The proper image for this relationship is not a circle with the *Yishuv* in the center and the Diaspora at the periphery, but rather an ellipse with two foci.

Contemporary Reform thought seems to flirt with both positions. The *Centenary Perspective*[13] avoids any suggestion of "centrality" for Israel. This document affirms that Israel provides "unique opportunities for Jewish self-expression," that it has made important cultural and psychological contributions to American Reform Jews, and that it is "vital to the welfare of Judaism everywhere." Nevertheless, there is no compromise on the importance or authenticity of the Diaspora. Our "tradition" mandates the creation of strong Jewish communities wherever we live; a "genuine Jewish life is possible in any land, each community developing its own particular character and determining its Jewish responsibilities." The operative model is apparently one of partnership and "fruitful dialogue" between equals.

The liturgy of the movement reflects an apparent ambivalence on the subject, encapsulated by the use of two alternative *chatimot* for "*Retseh.*" It is not difficult to find language that repudiates the notion of Israelo-centrism: "Wherever we live, wherever we seek You — in this land, in Zion restored, in all lands — you are our God"; "We give thanks for the return of our people to Zion. ... We give thanks for freedom in this land, and we pray for the peoples of every continent. ... Praised be the strength and love that makes every land and people grow toward justice and right." Yet both *Gates of Prayer* and *Gates of Repentance* restored some of the liturgical language that conveyed a sense of the centrality of Israel and Jerusalem in traditional worship: a version of the "Jerusalem Benediction" of the daily *Tefila*; the "*ve-al Yerushalayim*" conclusion of some versions of "*Hashkiveinu*"; the phrase "*simcha le-artsecha ve-sason le-irecha*" in the second paragraph of "*Uvechen.*" Sometimes the Israelo-centrism of the restored traditional Hebrew is modified in the English rendition (e.g., *Gates of Prayer*, p. 137 *et al.*; *Gates of Repentance*, p. 36); occasionally language suggesting the centrality of Zion appears in English without any basis in the original Hebrew (*Gates of Prayer*, p. 156). In comparison with their respective predecessors, both *Gates of Prayer* and *Gates of Repentance* appear to have laid the groundwork for a Reform affirmation of the centrality of the

Land, if not the State, of Israel. But the message is by no means unequivocal.

More recently, however, a CCAR resolution, acknowledging "diverse meanings embedded within the term 'Centrality,'" has affirmed "the historic centrality of the State of Israel for the Jewish people."[14] The force of the phrase "historic centrality" is anything but clear — perhaps the ambiguity was intentional — but a plausible exegesis may be based on the discussion of "centrality" in the ARZA Platform, a text that bears witness to some anguished wrestling with the religious implications of affirming the "centrality of Israel." As a Zionist body, ARZA had to make peace with this phrase; as part of a religious movement, it had to insist that God, Torah, and the Jewish people as a whole take precedence over any land and any state.

The latter assertion appears first: it is "the union of God, Torah and the People Israel" that is the "central element in Jewish life." "In the perspective of our people's encounter with the Eternal, the unity of the inseparable components [God, Torah, and People] has been indispensable." However, "in the perspective of our encounter with history, confined to time and space alone, the central event in current Jewish life is Israel, which contains far-reaching and profound implications for our faith." In that "historic" context, "the State does occupy a special central place in Jewish life."

This is apparently the clue for understanding the force of the CCAR reference to "the historic centrality of the State of Israel for the Jewish people." If we remove God and Torah from the discussion for the moment and think only of empirical realities, then Israel is central. The "centrality of Israel" is thereby affirmed — at the cost of precisely that highly problematic bifurcation of the late 18th and early 19th century: between the religious and the ethnic dimensions of Jewish identity. In fact, there is a curious reversal of the strategy adopted by Moses Mendelssohn (and German Orthodox rabbis in his wake) in response to the charge that the hope for return to the Land of Israel made it impossible to consider the Jews as legitimate candidates for full citizenship. They claimed that in the private religious domain, "Israel" might be central, but in the public, empirical, historical domain it was not, having no practical effect on the behavior of Jews in the countries where they lived.[15] The ARZA/CCAR contention is the opposite: in the private religious domain, Israel cannot be central; in the practical, empirical domain, it is.

What remains unclear, however, is just how it is possible to affirm the "centrality of Israel," even in this somewhat restricted sense, without reducing the Diaspora to a status of marginality and inferiority. The largest and most influential Jewish community in history is unlikely to be content with a role on the periphery of contemporary Jewish life or the task of providing financial and political support for a drama unfolding somewhere else. Nor are most rabbis prepared to concede that their work in the Diaspora has been relegated to a holding action for Jews of minimal commitment, fostering a largely vicarious Jewishness dependent for its vitality on a nation far away. Different models — the two foci of an ellipse, the two strands of the double helix, the two sides of the coin — capture the self-image of American Jewry more than the model of the circle and language of centrality.[16] Such alternative models are clearly compatible with contemporary Reform thought; whether they pass muster as a legitimate option in the spectrum of contemporary Zionist positions remains to be determined.

Whatever its usefulness as an ideological touchstone, *centrality* is still a vague term. It may well be argued that debates over the word are sterile, the more important question being where Israel actually stands in the hierarchy of contemporary American Reform Jewish values. But here there is a welter of conflicting evidence. A case could be made that, practically speaking, support for Israel remains the quintessential expression of modern Jewish allegiance. Nothing on the local scene inspires such philanthropic generosity or galvanizes such concerted political action. Few congregational events have as much impact as the tour of Israel led by the rabbi. Israel serves as the prime focus of Jewish pride, the paramount justification for Hebrew language study, the major protagonist in the mythos of contemporary Jewish history. It is the place to which children are sent when the synagogue has failed to "turn them on" to their Jewishness; it is used as a last resort in the sometimes desperate hope that they will forget their Gentile lover, stop using drugs, abandon a cult. It has become the primary test for political loyalties: no candidate perceived as anything less than fervently pro-Israel can hope for significant support among Reform or other Jews.

While some view this as entirely proper, others favor a diminution of the emphasis on Israel's role in American Reform. This position is not so much the legacy of an earlier generation's anti-Zionism, but rather the expression of other concerns: both problems with Israel itself — distress over a series of political blunders and scandals committed by Israeli governments of the 1980s, exasperation about the increasing militancy of Israeli political extremism and religious fanaticism, and anger over the prolonged second-class status of the Israeli Reform movement — and, perhaps most important, fear that over-reliance on Israel is leading to an empty vicariousness in American Jewish experience. Relevant evidence for determining the actual place of Israel in the hierarchy of contemporary Reform Jewish values is readily at hand. One can easily look at the proportion of the UAHC and HUC-JIR budgets, or the proportion of charitable donations by American Reform Jews, devoted to Israel-related programs. One can quickly determine the proportion of educational curricula and congregational programming bound up with Israel. But some of the more interesting tests would require investigation. A rabbi's choice of topics for High Holiday sermons reveals an important decision about priorities: it would be intriguing to find out what percentage of High Holiday sermon-time over the past 15 years was spent discussing matters relating to Israel; or what percentage of debating time at CCAR conventions was devoted to Israel-related resolutions; or what percentage of vacation and sabbatical time rabbis spend in Israel. Answers to such questions might tell us more about "centrality" than any purely ideological debate.[17]

Concrete and immediate issues compel some clarification of Israel's importance in the decision-making process of American Jews. For example, should Soviet Jewish emigrés be brought directly to Israel, or should they be given full freedom of choice in the selection of their new home? Israel's pressing need for immigration is buttressed by the claim that a diversion of Soviet emigration from Israel to the United States might jeopardize the chances of future applicants. These considerations have apparently been outweighed by an instinctive commitment to freedom of choice, a reluctance on the part of rabbis who do not live in Israel to tell Soviet Jews that they should, and the possibility of strengthening American Jewry by the infusion of "new blood." The issue has not been addressed by the CCAR in Resolutions or Committee Reports, but the sentiment against directing emigrants to Israel regardless of their personal preference seems clear.

A second test case might be the choice of alliances within the American Christian community. The strongest unquestioning support for the State of Israel and the policies of its government has come in recent years from evangelical circles. But these are the Christians most likely to view American Jews as spiritually blighted targets for their "witness," and their vision of American society is one that few, if any, Reform Jews could endorse. Praising them for their support of Israel runs the risk of enhancing their stature on the domestic scene; attacking them for their social agenda runs the risk of jeopardizing support that Israel badly needs. On the other hand, the mainstream and liberal Protestant denominations have been long-standing partners in religious dialogue and social action; they are most likely to respect an authentic Jewish identity. But they are often quite critical of Israeli positions and policies. Does this area of tension justify sacrificing an important alliance on domestic issues? A position on issues such as these will flesh out the real meaning of "centrality" for American Reform Jews.

If Israel is used as a catalyst for energies that can no longer be inspired by Torah, worship, and social action at home, then it certainly has become central in Jewish life, but not in a sense many rabbis would consider to be ideal. Yet the effort to cultivate stronger commitments to an agenda of parochial American Jewish concerns — spirituality, intensive study of traditional texts, and the pursuit of a just society — in short, the effort to replace vicarious with authentic Jewishness, might conceivably undermine the loyalties upon which Israel may some day depend. It is a juggling act, and the proper balance keeps shifting.

The Ingathering of the Jewish People Through *Aliya*

Aliya is certainly related to the question of the centrality of Israel, but it raises independent issues as well. Here, too, a spectrum of positions is refracted by traditional sources. Whether or not it is a *mitzvah* to live in the Land of Israel is a classical dispute involving an intricate interplay of exegetical problems, historical forces, and ideological commitments. This debate is not exhausted by a simple alternative. Those who claimed that it is a divine commandment were faced with additional decisions. First, they had to decide whether it was merely one of 613, on the same level as all others, or whether it was somehow of greater import and significance than the others. The statement "Dwelling in the Land of Israel is equal to all of the [other] divine commandments" (Sifrei on Deut. 12:29), though similar to other homiletical hyperboles, implies something unique about this precept.

It was also possible to maintain that the commandment to live in the Land was in abeyance, just as the various commandments relating to the sacrifices in the Temple. Such a position was apparently taken by Hayyim ben Hananel ha-Kohen (ca. 1150-1200); according to the Tosafot, he argued that, at present, "living in the Land of Israel is not a religious obligation at all, owing to the difficulty or impossibility of fulfilling many of the precepts attached to the soil."[18] According to this analysis, the commandment applied when the Temple was in existence and Jews had a state with a majority of the population; now historical circumstances have released Jews from this obligation until messianic times.

Others believed that there was no such commandment at all. Maimonides did not include any precept to live in the Land in his enumeration of 613 commandments, for which he was taken to task by Nahmanides and others. Some authorities went a step further, describing the decision to live in the Land of Israel in negative terms, at least in pre-messianic times. A dramatic formulation of this view was given by the great third-century Babylonian amora Rav Judah bar Ezekiel (d. 299), founder of the Pumbedita Academy (Ket. 1106-111a):

> Whoever goes up from Babylon to the Land of Israel transgresses a positive commandment, for it is said in Scripture, "They shall be carried to Babylon, and there they shall be, until the day that I remember them, says the Lord" (Jer. 27:22).

As his disciple R. Zera points out, the actual proof text is rather weak: it is taken not from the Torah but from the Prophets, in context it is more plausibly read not as a commandment about the Jewish people but as a prophecy about the vessels of ministry, and, at most, it can apply to the community of Babylonia. But it is clear evidence of an anti-*aliya* ideology in striking tension with the Tannaitic proclamations of a century earlier.

Indeed, when the proof text shifts to the Song of Songs, Rav Judah appears to be on even firmer ground. True, it is an exegesis of a poetic passage that seems to be far removed from the concreteness of commandment: "I adjure you, O daughters of Jerusalem ... that you awaken not, nor stir up love, until it please" (Song 2:7). But the appropriateness of this interpretation is not challenged by Zera. Conceding that it prohibits any movement of mass *aliya* in pre-messianic times, he argues against Rav Judah only that it does not preclude an individual from going to live in the Land. As this verse was not limited to the Babylonian community, it had sustained repercussions, forming the basis of the quietistic ideology of Diaspora that was for centuries widely prevalent in Jewish life.

The position of the Reform movement on *aliya* reflects the hesitations of American Zionism. Jerusalem has been restored to Reform liturgy, but the "Ingathering of the Exiles" remains alien. Neither the petition to be gathered "from the four corners of the earth" nor the characterization of God as the one who "gathers the dispersed of your people Israel" has been incorporated into the seventh benediction of the *Amida*, which instead, as its commentator noted, expresses the hope for "universal freedom."[19] The category of Exile is universalized, divorced from a geographical component, and possibly reduced to a metaphor: "Let every wanderer come home from the bitterness of exile." "Next year in Jerusalem" is not to be said at the culmination of Yom Kippur; it

appears at the end of the Reform Haggadah, but with an explanation that seems to shift from the geographical to a metaphorical-
spiritual sense of Jerusalem: "Still we affirm that all people will
rejoice together in the Zion of love and peace."[20]

The CCAR has on several occasions designated *aliya* as "an
option within the diverse expressions of Reform Judaism," and in
this context deemed it worthy of "encouragement."[21] The most
recent statement modifies the formulation slightly: *aliya* is a
"legitimate option within the spectrum of Reform Zionist
beliefs";[22] the minor strengthening in the word *legitimate* would
appear to be offset by the addition of *Zionist*, which might be
viewed as limiting the assertion to one component of the movement (Reform Zionism) rather than applying to the movement as a
whole. In any case, these statements, anything but a bold call to
aliya, actually seem to be somewhat defensive. By incorporating
the decision to live in Israel within the sacrosanct category of
diversity and freedom of choice, the Conference asserts that *olim*
have not betrayed the ideals of Reform Judaism, but it does not
suggest that *aliya* is a goal toward which Reform Jews might
aspire. The unresolved intellectual and spiritual challenges posed
by this issue are recognized by a statement affirming the "need to
confront openly Aliya as an aspect of Reform ideology. ... As a
maturing movement, we can no longer afford to treat such fundamental issues uncritically."[23]

Explicating the second principle of the Jerusalem Program, the
ARZA Platform makes the following points:

1. Historically, many Jews made *aliya* out of "profound religious and idealistic conviction."
2. Today, "the State of Israel also requires *aliya* for its survival
   and security."
3. *Aliya* is needed from North America, and particularly from
   the Reform movement, and "should be encouraged."
4. The principle of *aliya* is not incompatible with the
   "continuation of a viable American Jewry."

It is worth noting that the primary rationale in this statement is
pragmatic and utilitarian: *aliya* by American Reform Jews
strengthens Israel as a whole and the Israeli Reform movement in
particular; it solidifies the bonds between Israel and American
Jewry and brings the social consciousness of Reform Judaism to
the Jewish State. Nothing is said about *aliya* as a religious act
within the context of Reform. Those who elect *aliya* do something
useful to the State and the Reform movement; there is no suggestion that they are fulfilling a central Jewish value or obligation.

The *Centenary Perspective* focuses more on the individual's
motivation: "We encourage *aliya* for those who wish to find

maximum personal fulfillment in the cause of Zion." Perhaps the
ambiguity in this formulation is intentional: it could be understood
to mean that maximum personal fulfillment can be found only in
the cause of Zion, or that this is one of many possible ways in
which such fulfillment can be found. In either case, the emphasis
on "personal fulfillment" is reminiscent of an earlier decade. The
more interesting question is not whether any individual can find
maximum personal fulfillment in Israel, but whether anyone
within American Reform would argue that *aliya* is a necessary
(though surely not sufficient) condition for a "maximal Jewish
life."[24]

As far as I know, it is only in a certificate prepared by ARZA
for new *olim* that *aliya* is characterized in religious terms. Not
only is it the "highest ideal of the Zionist movement"; it is also the
fulfillment of "the Biblical injunction: 'Your children shall return
to their homeland' (Jer. 31:16)." One might quibble with the term
injunction: the biblical context is clearly one of prophecy, not
commandment; it speaks of what will happen, not what a Jew
must do, and this distinction is critical in the legal literature.
Nevertheless, the absence of a strong biblical base is not fatal.
The certificate represents a clear position, and it highlights the
question, which remains to be directly addressed, whether *aliya*
ought to be included in the category of *mitzvah* as understood by
Reform.

There is also the practical side of the issue. The operative word
in CCAR resolutions, the ARZA Platform, and the *Centennial
Perspective*, is *encourage*. Some might question whether this
word, surely not the strongest to begin with, is an honest reflection of reality — whether the movement in general, and the rabbinate, in particular, does indeed "encourage" *aliya*. Despite its
concentration on Israel, Reform educational curriculum hardly
presents *aliya* as a live option, let alone as a desideratum. ARZA
has prepared a certificate, but there is no appropriate ritual or
liturgy for the Reform Jew who decides to live in Israel. *Olim*
from the movement are rarely recognized and celebrated as
embodiments of its success; they are often quickly forgotten once
they disappear from the roster of their American synagogues.
There seems to be some concern about the possibility of exposing
the *oleh* to the potential "dangers" of secularism and Orthodoxy in
Israel. As for the rabbis, it would be revealing to investigate how
many, in looking over their sermons, could point to a single passage in which they "encouraged" *aliya*. After all, it is not easy to
encourage an act of Jewish commitment that the "encouragers"
themselves are not prepared to undertake.

This last point has been sharply addressed by Edgar E. Siskin, who noted the extremely limited number of American Reform rabbis, compared with Conservative and Orthodox colleagues, who have made *aliya*, even after retirement. His mordant conclusion bears repeating:

> Even those eloquent colleagues who have made a career of Zionist advocacy seem blocked when it comes to forsaking the golah. They may yearn for the Promised Land but only from the heights of a cosy suburban Pisgah. They are like Agar in Melville's *Clarel*, who pines for the Holy Land but stays at home embroidering a cloth which bears the words (in Hebrew), "If I forget thee, O Jerusalem." Each letter stitched with love, of course.[25]

Everyone knows the arguments. "I can make a better contribution to Jewish life here. I must not abandon my people, even for my own fulfillment as a Jew. How can I live in a place where my status as a rabbi is not honored, or even recognized? What would I do there: teach Hebrew? The economic sacrifice would be devastating." Yet the fact remains that a small number of Reform rabbinical *olim* have found "personal fulfillment," a richer Jewish life, and opportunities to help build a movement and a nation. What does it say about the CCAR's resolutions that there have not been more?

While the Reform movement has no official liturgical recognition or celebration of *aliya*, it does have a liturgy, in *Gates of the House*, for those about to visit Israel. This raises the question of the religious significance of such a visit. While the term *pilgrimage* is often used in this context, it should be clear that the modern tourist, even one who visits Israel during a holiday season, is in a different category from the *oleh le-regel* of the First and Second Commonwealth periods. The "pilgrim" of ancient times went to Jerusalem in fulfillment of an explicit injunction of the Torah, in order to observe the festivals in a manner possible only in the Temple. The commandment was deemed to apply only when the Temple was in existence. During the talmudic period and the early Middle Ages, by contrast, merely visiting the Land of Israel, as opposed to going to live there, was not considered to be an obligation, or even a particularly high value for a Jew.

By a process that has not been thoroughly investigated, a new conception emphasizing the value of a visit to the Land of Israel began to take hold in the High Middle Ages. Many opposed this view from a traditionalist standpoint. Joseph ben Moses of Trani (1569-1639) condemned the new conception: "If he is not able to live there, what value is there in his going there? All the praises of the Land of Israel apply to living there, not to going there with the

intention of returning [to the Diaspora]."[26] A similar position was
taken in a responsum by Solomon Freehof to the following question: "A couple saved for years to visit Israel for a month. But
now they plan to use the money for the college expenses of their
children. Have they the right to do so? Is it not a supreme, religious duty to go to Palestine?" After reviewing the legal literature
on the religious status of settling in the Land, Rabbi Freehof concluded that "there is not, as far as I know, any authoritative opinion at all to the effect that a brief visit is to be considered a religious duty."[27]

Yet the CCAR has recently affirmed by resolution its view that
"tourism to Israel is the fulfillment of a mitzvah."[28] The resolution
calls upon colleagues "to continue to teach" this, thereby implying
that — Freehof to the contrary notwithstanding — it is standard
doctrine. This position, characterizing *aliya* as a "legitimate
option" and tourism as the "fulfillment of a *mitzvah*," though not
entirely surprising given the realities of American Jewish life,
looks rather strange from the perspective either of Jewish law or
of Zionist theory. Does the Conference really mean to affirm that
the Reform Jew who visits Israel on a 10-day deluxe tour has done
something of greater religious significance than the Reform Jew
who settles in Jerusalem or Yahel?

The Strengthening of the State and
the Prophetic Ideals of Justice and Peace

The third principle of the Jerusalem Program brings us beyond
Eretz Yisrael and the Jewish community settled upon it to the
State of Israel. An earlier statement, ratified by the 23rd Zionist
Congress of 1951, spoke only of "the consolidation of the State of
Israel"; the addition, drawing from language of the Declaration of
Independence, affirms something substantive about the nature of
the State. While it could be argued that a secular, democratic state
with a majority of Jewish citizens in *Eretz Yisrael* is both unprecedented and unanticipated in traditional Jewish literature, contemporary Zionism proclaims that the new body politic of 1948 is
organically bound up with values that come from the biblical past.

But for anyone conversant with traditional Jewish discourse,
this formulation carries deeper resonance. A "State of Israel"
founded on prophetic ideals is likely to be considered the fulfillment of the ancient prophecies. What, then, is the religious significance of the establishment of the State? Does the modern State of
Israel signify God's presence in history; is its role in the divine
plan fundamentally different from that of the states of Albania, Sri
Lanka, or Bahrain? Is there a connection between the events of

1948 and 1967 and the traditional concept of messianic redemption, when the "prophetic values of justice and peace" would finally prevail.

Most classical Zionists would have been surprised or even shocked by such a claim. They viewed their movement as the antithesis of traditional messianism, which they understood to entail a patient waiting until God would initiate the miraculous ingathering of the exiles. The Zionists' insistence on the priority of human initiative and political activism, and their gravitation toward socialistic economic structures, a parliamentary form of government, and modern technology, set them apart from any models in the tradition. They saw Zionism as a purely secular enterprise. Any role conceded to God or prophecy would demean their own achievement.

The fundamentally secular character of Zionism was one premise on which political Zionists and Orthodox anti-Zionists could agree. They simply drew antithetical conclusions from the same starting point. Orthodox opponents dismissed the movement as, at best, devoid of any positive content: "Let no one imagine that the redemption and salvation of Israel will come through the Zionists."[29] At worst it was a perversion of true Jewish values, a violation of talmudic injunctions, a defiance of God's plan. Some actually identified it as the work of Satan, a sin of such magnitude that it occasioned the most horrifying divine punishment of the Jewish people in history.

Other thinkers with deep religious commitments repudiate the suggestion of any religious significance to the State of Israel for different reasons. One of the last pieces written by the theologian Arthur Cohen argued that "Zionism is virtually without internal, substantive, or essential religious significance."[30] The alternative position, he maintained, entailed the obvious dangers of a politicized eschatology, in which fanaticism and intolerance would be validated by an appeal to God's will. The proposition that God was actively involved in history also entailed an unacceptable corollary: "If God is the revealer of our redemption, so God must be the agent of our destruction [during the Holocaust]."[31]

Even before the beginning of the movement, however, rabbis such as Judah Alkalai and Zevi Hirsch Kalischer argued that the return of the Jewish people to the Land of Israel and the establishment of institutions to facilitate settlement would be the first steps toward *Ge-ula*, which had to be taken on human initiative before any further progress in the redemptive drama could be made. When the Zionist movement was established, Orthodox supporters vehemently repudiated the feasibility of creating any secular Jewish nationalist movement divorced from the religious tradition. What was happening in the Land of Israel had to have significance beyond the surface level of political machinations; it had to be connected with the ultimate redemption.

This outlook was embodied in the formulation of the Chief Rabbinate's Prayer for the State of Israel. Modern Israel is called the "beginning of the sprouting of our redemption," a phrase which, despite its qualification, unmistakably identifies the State as a protagonist in *Heilsgeschichte* as well as in *Realpolitik*. Much more explicit are the spokesmen for Gush Emunim. Zvi Yehudah Kook and his followers considered the State of Israel to be the Third Commonwealth foretold by the Prophets, and the period after June 1967 no longer the beginning but the "middle of the redemption."[32] For settlers in Tekoa and elsewhere in the resonant hills of Judea and Samaria, it is obvious that their own labors fulfill the biblical prophecies of return, that present events bear witness to the tracing of God's finger on the contours of history.

Conflicting Views on Israel's Religious and Redemptive Significance

Having come to terms with Zionism, the Reform movement has yet to take a clear-cut stand on the religious/redemptive significance of the State of Israel. The literature of the past two generations reflects an ambivalence on precisely this point, a shifting back and forth in response to changing conditions. Early Reform Zionists tended to justify the movement in secular, pragmatic terms, arguing the need for a secure refuge for Jews facing the dangers of resurgent anti-Semitism. A distinction is unmistakably drawn in the Columbus Platform of 1937, the first positive statement on Zionist aspirations taken by the CCAR. The "rehabilitation of Palestine" offers "the promise of renewed life for many of our brethren"; all Jews are obligated to help build this Jewish homeland as a "haven of refuge for the oppressed" and as a "center of Jewish culture and spiritual life." But while the legacies of Herzl and Ahad Ha'am meet happily in this sentence, no religious significance is conceded to the enterprise. That is reserved for the "mission" in the Diaspora: our historic task is "to cooperate with all men in the establishment of the Kingdom of God, of universal brotherhood, justice, truth and peace on earth. This is our Messianic goal."[33]

In the debates of the 1930s and 1940s, however, a new emphasis can be discerned. One of the most powerful anti-Zionist arguments was the essentially secular and often militantly anti-religious nature of the movement. Responding to this attack, Reform Zionist spokesmen found it helpful to claim a religious dimension.

The prophetic promises of restoration — in Jeremiah 32 and Amos 9 — provided effective rhetoric in describing the achievements of the *Yishuv*.[34] It seemed natural, almost obvious, for rabbis to use such language in the context of the Zionist enterprise.

Yet this view has not been incorporated into the movement's liturgy. The redemptive significance of *Medinat Yisrael* is occasionally hinted,[35] but clear affirmations are withheld. Unlike the new *siddur* of the Conservative movement, Reform liturgy does not describe the State of Israel as the beginning of redemption. Even the *siddur* of the Hebrew Union College in Jerusalem, which incorporates much of the language of the Chief Rabbinate's Prayer for *Medinat Yisrael*, omits the crucial phrase "*reshit tzemichat geulateinu*." In the *Gates of Repentance* Yom Kippur Afternoon Service, the liturgy relating to Israel is entitled "Rebirth," while the following section, "Redemption," is entirely universalistic, and entirely in the future. On this issue, the *Centenary Perspective* follows the Columbus Platform rather closely. The State of Israel "demonstrates what a united people can accomplish in history" and serves as a "warrant for human hope," but it is not linked with the messianic vision; that is reserved for the "hope that humanity will be redeemed," and no role is suggested for the State of Israel in this context.

Various reasons for this stance might be suggested. The legacy of the doctrine of mission is still strong. As an essentially Diaspora movement, Reform remains committed to the pursuit of the messianic age where we are. An affirmation that Israel is the "beginning of our redemption" might be viewed as denying any central role in the messianic drama for Jews among the nations. Furthermore, Reform was historically committed to an activist messianism, emphasizing the importance of human initiative in bringing near the messianic age rather than passively waiting for God's own time. The corollary would be that on this issue Alkalai and Kalischer and those who insisted that human beings have to take the first steps were right, and the Orthodox opponents of Zionism were wrong. But today, the mantle of Zionist messianic activism is claimed by political forces most Reform Jews find quite antipathetic. There is deep suspicion of those who act as if they have the Messiah in their back pocket. Once the establishment of the State is vouchsafed some messianic significance, it is not clear how to guard against the potential for fanaticism and intolerance so frequently bound up with triumphalist political messianism. A logical middle ground between the Gush Emunim conception of Israel as semi-realized eschatology with God's finger writ large, and the militantly secular repudiation of all connections with the Jewish tradition, seems elusive. Given the realities of contemporary Middle Eastern politics, keeping a safe distance from all messianic claims often looks like the most prudent course.[36]

Despite the hesitations about incorporating modern Israel into the redemptive drama, even as prologue, the Reform movement is committed to affirming religious significance to the establishment of the State. In a sense, it has gone further than Orthodoxy in drawing practical conclusions from this premise. Reform was the first American Jewish movement to incorporate a service for Israel Independence Day into its prayerbook, thereby marking this day as an official part of its religious calendar. *Gates of the Seasons* affirms that "it is a *mitzvah* for every Jew to mark Yom ha-Atsma-ut." Orthodoxy is obviously less amenable to the idea of new *mitzvot*, and except for the special liturgy which was needed to substitute for the traditional "Prayer on Behalf of the State," it has shown reluctance to adapt its liturgy to the new realities of Jewish national sovereignty and a united and rebuilt Jerusalem.[37]

Yet decisions taken by rabbinical bodies are not automatically translated into practice, and it might well be asked how deeply the commitment to a religious assessment of the State has taken root in Reform. The number of congregations that actually observe Yom ha-Atsma-ut not just with a special program on the nearest Friday night but with a religious service on the proper day cannot be very large. In the absence of any commonly recognized Independence Day ritual comparable to the reading of the *Megilla* or the kindling of lights, it will certainly not be easy to elevate the occasion to the level of Purim or Chanuka. The basic context for American Jewish observance of Yom ha-Atsma-ut is communal and secular, rather than synagogal and religious; one consequence is that rabbis are rarely in center-stage. Whether this is a healthy expression of the instincts of the people or the symptom of a malady to be resisted remains open to debate.

Alternative Visions of an Ideal Israel

The language of the Zionist affirmation raises other important questions about the nature of the State. When measured against the "prophetic ideals of justice and peace," most would agree that the reality of contemporary Israel falls painfully short. But despite widespread dissatisfaction about the current condition of Israeli society, concrete proposals for change lack consensus and generally meet with vehement opposition. Setting aside any consideration of the plausibility of fundamental change (and thereby avoiding the pitfalls of political analysis and prognostication), let us consider the most coherent visions of an Israel radically different from the present reality, and the implications of such transformations for Reform support.

One powerful configuration of forces includes all those who would like to see Israel become "more Jewish." They decry the extent to which Israeli society has been suffused by some of the most decadent of modern Western values: secularism, consumerism, hedonism, all conveniently symbolized by the Tel Aviv beachfront on Friday night. They are incensed by widespread public disregard of the sancta of traditional Jewish life, particularly the Sabbath and Holy Days, and the dietary laws. They agonize over a generation of Israeli youth, products of the secular educational system, who are ignorant of, and hostile toward, all expressions of Jewish religious experience. They are therefore committed to maximizing traditional values and traditional observance in the society, in order to make Israel truly, as Ahad Ha'am once wrote in criticizing Herzl (but with a very different idea in mind), "not merely a State of Jews but a truly Jewish State."[38]

One might assume that Reform, as a religious movement in Judaism, would be highly sympathetic to such a program. The problem is not so much the nature of the goals, but the means of achieving them. For the quickest and most effective way of changing behavior, and perhaps even values, is through legislation, and thus through political coercion. From the perspective of most Israeli Orthodox, it is not unreasonable to prohibit Jews from keeping their businesses open on the Sabbath or from raising pigs; after all, it is the function of the law to embody the underlying values of the society. Of course there is a sacrifice of personal freedom. Laws prohibiting segregation in this country impinged on the personal freedom of many citizens in the South. It is a trade-off; to the Orthodox, the toll that full individual freedom takes on the Jewish character of the State is simply too high.

At what point, however, would the toll on individual freedom taken by legislation to ensure a more "Jewish" Israel be too high? What would be the next step in ensuring greater Sabbath observance? Prohibiting the operation of all publicly sponsored transportation, radio, television, entertainment, and so forth throughout the country? Regulating the behavior of individuals, by prohibiting not only public transportation but all non-emergency driving on the Sabbath? Behind the appealing vision of a more "Jewish" Israel lurks the specter of a Khomeini-like "theocracy." In the context of the Middle East, it is not obvious how to move toward the first without opening the door toward the second.

The most radical program for the "Judaization" of Israel is the platform on which Meir Kahane was elected to the Knesset.

Whatever the exact extent of his political support, Kahane has raised claims that can no longer be cavalierly dismissed by branding them as "racist," justifiable as this epithet may be. Kahanism is not merely a political doctrine but a version of Judaism that claims exclusivity and therefore demands response. His platform is justified not merely on pragmatic but on "Jewish" grounds: "authentic, Torah Judaism" teaches that Gentiles must not be permitted to live in Jerusalem, that non-Jews may never be tolerated in Israel as equal citizens but only in a status of subservience to their Jewish overlords, that Jews are permitted to engage in random, preemptive acts of terror against non-Jews in order to intimidate against attacks; that sexual relations between Jews and Gentiles should be legislatively banned and judicially punished. Values such as democracy, toleration, and liberalism are the legacy of either "Hellenism" or the Enlightenment — not merely alien to Judaism, but antithetical to it. This position strikes at the heart of mainstream American Zionism, which often identified both the Jewish spirit and the Zionist enterprise with American democratic values. It also strikes at the foundations of the self-conception of most American Reform Jews.

This is not the place to assess the legitimacy of the claim to represent "authentic Judaism." The question here is the implications of the Kach platform for the relationship of American Reform Jews to Israel. Kahane raises the classic dilemma of the appropriate response of a democracy to those who exploit its liberties and rights in order to undermine and overthrow it. While it remains unlikely that his base of support can be substantially broadened, his effect may be in making other — less extreme, but similarly distasteful — right-wing views seem moderate and acceptable by comparison. Or he might play a role similar (*mutatis mutandis*) to that of Norman Thomas in American politics, watching important elements of his platform taken over by larger parties and eventually implemented. It is worth contemplating what would be the Reform Zionist obligation toward "strengthening the State" if Kahane's vision of Israel were ever to prevail.

This specter of a "rabbinic ayatollism," or worse, fuels the antithetical vision of Israel: one that would become more secular, more liberal, more tolerant, an Israel transformed into a fully pluralistic, secular democracy with complete separation of "Church and State." In order to be theoretically coherent, this model of Israel would require that Jews renounce any special status in the country, other than being the majority ethnic group. There would be no governmentally sponsored Chief Rabbinate, no laws imposing any modes of traditional religious behavior, no intrusion of

Jewish law into the realms of marriage and divorce. Ideologically, there would have to be a total severing of the nexus between Zionism and Judaism, a repudiation of links with the traditional ideal of redemption and territorial claims drawn from the Bible, and a reconstruction of Israel on the basis not of the Jewish religious myth but squarely on the values and insights of the Enlightenment.[39]

Much about this vision is attractive, particularly as an alternative to the "theocratic" model. But what about its costs? Few visitors fail to be moved by the aura of Sabbath peace and tranquility that descends upon the hills of Jerusalem as the sun reaches the horizon on Friday afternoon. But this special character of Jerusalem is, after all, the result of coercion, a legal mandate, on religious grounds, that businesses close and buses stop. Without such coercion, Orthodox Jews would still refrain from work, but many Jews who might prefer to observe Shabbat would feel the constraints of economic competition to keep their shops open. With the buses running, much of Jerusalem would be as noisy on the Sabbath as on the rest of the week. Whether it is worth sacrificing such intangibles for the ideal of a fully civil libertarian Israel is at least open to debate.

The logic of a totally secular democratic Israel would probably require repeal of the Law of Return, one of the most obvious expressions of the "Jewishness" of the State. This would at least defuse one politically explosive imbroglio over "Who is a Jew?" But it would also make possible a future scenario when the Soviet Union might again open the doors to large-scale emigration and an Israeli government would impose a rigid immigration quota because of an economic slump. It would make conceivable a return to the situation in the 1930s, when Jews were able to leave Germany but no country in the world, including our own, was willing to accept them.

There is some question whether a government of Israel can really be "neutral" with regard to religion as the American government is mandated to be. An Israeli government that carried on business as usual on the Sabbath, an Israeli army or airline that served kosher food only by special arrangement, would probably be perceived, and with some justification, not as neutral, but as anti-religious. If the official institutions of the nation were identified with open violation of Jewish sancta and norms, not only Orthodox Jews but all Jews who take the tradition seriously might be the losers.

In conflicts over the role of religion in Israel, American Reform tends instinctively to side with the secularists. The reasons are obvious. Since the beginning of the State, the Orthodox estab-

lishment has fought a brutal campaign against all efforts to intro-
duce Reform as an alternative for Israeli Jews. The wounds from
those battles, and the legacy of ongoing discrimination and
second-class religious status, continue to rankle. Furthermore,
militant ultra-Orthodoxy is engaging in activities that can only
inspire revulsion within the Reform community: the stoning of
cars on Shabbat, the suppression of archaeological digs in areas
that might once have had graves, the vandalizing of bus stops
where lingerie is advertised. There is a legitimate resolve to resist
such behavior, lest more extreme positions be pressed. Finally,
there is an understandable tendency to apply positions drawn from
American realities to Israel. Here the Reform position has historically been allied with civil libertarian concerns, vigorously resist-
ing any hint of a breach in the famous "wall of separation."

Israeli issues, however, may sometimes require more than an
automatic lineup against the Orthodox. For example, the demand
that Israel's airline cease operations on the Sabbath imposes an
obvious loss of revenue and financial hardship, which must be
made up by Israeli taxpayers. From the secular side, it seems an
atavistic intrusion of ancient law into the totally inappropriate
realm of modern technology and rational corporate management,
another step toward the theocratic rule of the rabbis. But what
about the other side of the question?

There are at least two claims. First, there is a civil liberties
argument, similar to that made by Roman Catholics about publicly
subsidized abortion, that if El Al operated on Shabbat (and lost
money), Orthodox Jews would be forced to pay taxes to help sub-
sidize activities which violate their religious convictions. The second argument is on symbolic grounds: while Jews should be indi-
vidually free to choose to travel on Shabbat, any Jew sympathetic
to the tradition should empathize with the outrage felt by obser-
vant Israeli Jews at the thought that the airline universally identified with their country would openly violate Jewish law. How
would we react if the president of Israel scheduled a state banquet
for visiting American dignitaries on Yom Kippur? In cases such as
this, it may not be a matter of simple "right" and "wrong," but
rather a more complex conflict between two sets of values, both
of which should have some claim upon Reform Jews.

It is worth asking whether the Reform movement, in its necessary and legitimate struggle against the discriminatory power of
the Orthodox establishment and aggressive militancy of the ultra-
Orthodox fringes, needs to ally itself automatically and in all circumstances with the forces pushing for an Israel reconstructed in
the image of Western-style secular democracy. Many of the most
vociferous in the struggle against religious coercion are unalter-

ably hostile not only to Orthodox expansionism, but also to Jewish religious tradition and experience as a whole. Suspicious of the special ties between Israel and Diaspora Jewry, they abhor signs of awakening interest in Judaism within circles of secular Israeli youth. They defend the classical severance of Zionism from Judaism and trumpet the goal of normalcy devoid of any aspirations toward uniqueness or any hint of a messianic burden. In the conflict between polar extremes, choosing political alliances often means embracing one side because the other is unimaginable. The harder task is to resist the pressures for polarization, to stake out a middle ground between the extremes, and to identify partners in a coalition of those unwilling to be subsumed in either camp.

Between the two alternative visions of an ideal Israel lies the Israel of the past 40 years, with all the ambiguities, tensions, and internal contradictions of the "status quo." The ideological incoherence, the social cleavages, and the examples of injustice and inequity are painfully apparent. The question is whether massive movement in the direction of either greater "Jewishness" or greater secularism would be an improvement.

•

Historically, both Reform Judaism and Zionism were committed to an ending of *Galut* as traditionally understood — Reform through the transformation of the Diaspora environment in which Jews found themselves, Zionism through an abandonment of that environment. Today, in retrospect, the early optimism of both movements seems terribly naïve. The Reform belief that history was inexorably moving toward universal enlightenment and brotherhood, and the Zionist belief that the restoration of national sovereignty would eliminate the cause of anti-Jewish prejudice, have both been falsified by the unexpected yet irrefutable evidence of historical events.

The ideal of an "Israel founded on the prophetic ideals of justice and peace" can be seen as a wedding of the aspirations of both movements. Yet there are times when these values seem so far removed from reality that the very words take on a mordantly bitter taste. The distance from the vision of redemption looks considerably greater today than it did either in the wake of Emancipation or in 1948. God's presence in history, so palpably manifest in June of 1967, now seems much more paradoxical, as the ambiguous legacy of the Six-Day War unfolds. Whether the proper message today is to stay the course or to change direction is no longer a matter of certainty or consensus. "Reform Zionism" will never again be thought of as a contradiction in terms, as it once would have been, but it may well need to evolve as a complex and multivalent synthesis, devoid of predictable analyses and simple solutions.

NOTES

* This is a somewhat abbreviated version of an article submitted in early January 1988 for the CCAR Centennial Volume. Although the delay in publication may make several passages appear anachronistic, I believe that the basic arguments are in no need of modification.

[1] David Polish, *Renew Our Days: The Zionist Issue in Reform Judaism* (Jerusalem: World Zionist Organization, 1976); Howard Greenstein, *Turning Point: Zionism and Reform Judaism* (Missoula, Montana: Scholars Press, 1981).

[2] Ahad Ha'am, "The Negation of the Diaspora," in Arthur Hertzberg, *The Zionist Idea* (New York: Atheneum, 1975), henceforth: "Hertzberg," p. 270.

[3] Jacob Klatzkin, "Boundaries," in Hertzberg, p. 322.

[4] "A Debate on Zionism and Messianism," in Paul Mendes-Flohr and Jehuda Reinharz, editors, *The Jew in the Modern World* (Oxford and New York: Oxford University Press, 1980), p. 452.

[5] Ahad Ha'am, in Hertzberg, pp. 275-276; cf. Mordecai Kaplan in Etan Levine, ed., *Diaspora: Exile and the Contemporary Jewish Condition* (New York, 1986), p. 234.

[6] Simon Dubnow, "The Affirmation of the Diaspora," in *Nationalism and History* (Philadelphia: Jewish Publication Society, 1958), pp. 185-186.

[7] *Ibid.*, p. 187.

[8] *Ibid.*, p. 189.

[9] Harold Fisch, *The Zionist Revolution: A New Perspective* (New York: Shapolsky Books, 1978), p. 104.

[10] Simon Rawidowicz, *Studies in Jewish Thought* (Philadelphia: Jewish Publication Society, 1974), p. 15.

[11] *Ibid.*, p. 171.

[12] *Ibid.*, p. 402.

[13] "Reform Judaism: A Centenary Perspective," in Eugene Borowitz, *Reform Judaism Today*, Book 1: *Reform in the Process of Change* (New York: Behrman House, 1978), pp. xxiii-xxiv.

[14] *CCAR Yearbook* 93 (1983), p. 188; repeated in vol. 94 (1984), p. 145.

[15] Moses Mendelssohn, in Mendes-Flohr and Reinharz, p. 43; Barukh Mevorakh, "Ha-Emuna ba-Mashiach be-Pulmusei ha-Reforma ha-Rishon-im," *Zion* 34 (1969), pp. 197, 205, 213, and 215.

[16] As noted above, the "two foci of an ellipse" metaphor was popularized (and possibly originated) by Rawidowicz. The image of the "double-helix" was used by David Polish, "The Place of Israel in Reform Theology," Address to the UAHC 51st General Assembly, November 8, 1971. "Two sides of a coin" was suggested by Arnold Wolf in the context of the "Breira"

controversy. It is extremely difficult to be certain about the very first use of such phrases.

17 For an example of a revealing study of Reform High Holiday preaching on Israel, see Daniel Jeremy Silver, "What We Said about Lebanon," *Journal of Reform Judaism* 30:2 (Spring, 1983), pp. 20-37. By some standards, it would appear that Israel plays a rather small role in Reform Jewish life. Of the hundreds of responsa contained in the seven volumes of Solomon Freehof and the two recently published anthologies — including some that deal with cannibalism, sex-change operations, and cryobiology — only two deal directly with Israel-related issues: whether an Israeli flag is appropriate in the synagogue and whether visiting Israel is a religious obligation. It is perhaps revealing that the largest single category in the Index to the two volumes of *American Reform Responsa* — larger than "Cemetery," "Medical Ethics," and "Religious Practice" — is "Christians."

18 Tos. Ket. 110b, "Hu." See my article "The Land of Israel in Pre-Modern Jewish Thought," in Lawrence Hoffman, ed., *The Land of Israel: Jewish Perspectives* (Notre Dame, IN: University of Notre Dame Press, 1986), p. 193, and Ephraim Kanarfogel, "The 'Aliyah of Three Hundred Rabbis' in 1211: Tosafist Attitudes Toward Settling in the Land of Israel," *JQR* 76 (1986), pp. 200-201. This view is also articulated in Isaac de Leon's Megillat Esther to Maimonides' Sefer ha-Mitzvot, "Mitzvot she-Shakhach ha-Rambam kefi Da'at ha-Ramban," Positive Commandment 4.

19 See *Gates of Understanding* (New York: CCAR, 1977), p. 190.

20 *A Passover Haggadah* (New York: CCAR, 1974), p. 93. Roland Gittelsohn's statement, "We conclude our worship at the Pesach seder and on Yom Kippur, holiest day in our calendar, with the refrain... 'Next year in Jerusalem!'" is surprising: do Reform congregations actually do this? See "Partners in Destiny: Reform Judaism and Zionism" (New York: UAHC, 1984), p. 5.

21 *CCAR Yearbook* 93 (1983), p. 189; vol. 94 (1984), p. 145.

22 *CCAR Yearbook* 96 (1986), p. 215.

23 *CCAR Yearbook* 95 (1985), p. 245.

24 Note the formulation in the ARZA platform: "The Land of Israel ... was traditionally perceived as the place where Israel's Covenant with God could most fully be realized through the inspiration of the Torah." The characterization of Eretz Yisrael as the appropriate environment for maximal Jewish living is placed in the past: not endorsed as currently valid, nor suggested as a reason for aliya.

25 "Israel ... Anyone?" *Journal of Reform Judaism* 26:2 (Spring 1979), p. 23.

26 *Shu"t MaHaRYT*, I, nu. 134, cited in Israel Schepansky, *Eretz Yisrael be-Sifrut ha-Teshuvot* (Jerusalem: Mosad Ha-Rav Kook, 1966), I, 321; cf. I, 318.

27 Freehof, *Contemporary Reform Responsa* (Cincinnati: HUC Press, 1974), p. 73. The statement is too categorical; there are some later authorities who consider the visit to the Land of Israel in the category of mitzvah (see the conclusion of Hayyim Palache in *Nishmat Kol Chai*, I, nu. 50, p. 87 col. b). I

hope to explore the origins and development of this conception in a separate study.

28 *CCAR Yearbook* 96 (1986), p. 216.

29 "Statement of the Gerer Rebbe, 1901," cited in Michael Selzer, ed. *Zionism Reconsidered: The Rejection of Jewish Normalcy* (London: Macmillan, 1970), p. 70. The view of Zionism as the work of Satan, responsible for the Holocaust, has been argued most forcefully by the late Satmarer Rebbe Joel Teitelbaum in *Va-Yo'el Mosheh.*

30 Arthur Cohen, "Zionism and Theology," *Sh'ma* 17/324 (December 26, 1986), p. 26.

31 *Ibid.,* p. 27.

32 Zvi Yehudah Kook, cited by Uriel Tal, "Contemporary Hermeneutics and Self-Views on the Relationship between State and Land," in Hoffman, *The Land of Israel,* p. 333 n. 12. Cf. Amos Oz, *In the Land of Israel* (New York: Harcourt Brace Jovanovich, 1983), pp. 70-71; Ian S. Lustick, *For the Land and the Lord: Jewish Fundamentalism in Israel* (New York: Council on Foreign Relations, 1988), pp. 93-94.

33 "The Columbus Platform," in W. Gunther Plaut, *The Growth of Reform Judaism* (New York: World Union for Progressive Judaism, 1965), pp. 97-98.

34 See, e.g., "Are Zionism and Reform Judaism Incompatible?" Papers read at the 1943 Convention of the CCAR (New York: CCAR, 1943), p. 28 (Felix Levy), pp. 51-52 (David Polish). On the circumstances in which these papers were first delivered, see Polish, *Renew Our Days,* pp. 212-214.

35 One might find such a hint in the use of Ezekiel 37 (The Valley of Dry Bones) as the bridge between the Holocaust and Israel (*Gates of Prayer,* 597; *Gates of Repentance,* 443). The words "Let Your Torah go forth from Zion and Your word from Jerusalem" (*Gates of Prayer,* 42) are supposed to be an "allusion to the connection between Zion and the messianic hope, expressed by the reference to Zion and Jerusalem as a source of enlightenment to all humanity" (*Gates of Understanding,* p. 191). But it is a prayer for the future, not a comment on the rebirth of Israel.

36 See the comment on Arthur Cohen's above-mentioned article by Eric Yoffie, *Sh'ma* 17/324, December 26, 1986, p. 30: "the State has no theological meaning.... Such claims [of the contrary] constitute an extraordinary theological arrogance, and resemble the pseudo-messianism for which we have paid so dearly." For attempts to define a "middle ground" on this issue, see Arthur Green, "Finding God in an Israel that isn't Zion," *Sh'ma* 17/327 (February 6, 1987), pp. 54-56, and David Polish, "Israel: Some Halachic/ Theological Perspectives," *Journal of Reform Judaism* 31:1 (Winter 1984), pp. 44-59.

37 On the equivocation of the Chief Rabbinate regarding the use of Hallel for Yom ha-Atsma-ut and the modification of Tisha be-Av liturgy, see S. Zalman Abramov, *Perpetual Dilemma: Jewish Religion in the Jewish State* (Rutherford, NJ: Associated University Presses, 1976), pp. 245-258.

38 Ahad Ha'am in Hertzberg, p. 267. Considerable confusion has been engendered by the translation of the title of Herzl's Judenstaat as "The Jewish State."

[39] A provocative argument on behalf of this model of Israel has been made by James Diamond, *Homeland or Holy Land? The "Canaanite" Critique of Israel* (Bloomington, IN: University of Indiana Press, 1986), pp. 125-135.

THE NEXT CENTURY

Peter J. Rubinstein

Anniversaries are as much an occasion to consider the future as to celebrate the past. Certainly this is true for a 100th anniversary. The history of the first century of the Central Conference of American Rabbis was one of transformation. Upon entering our second century, our vision turns to the future, which we can expect to be as filled with change and challenge as has been the past.

This is not the first time special occasions have been used to consider the future. The practice began early in our movement. As early as 1841, a search for directions confounded our forebears. The subject of an essay offered by the *Culturverein* of Berlin was *"Was war, was ist, und was soll de Rabbinic sein?"* ("What Was, What Is, and What Shall the Rabbinate Be?").

The change in structure and content of the rabbinate was of great magnitude. It reflected a revolutionary shift within the Jewish community.

Our forebears were aflame with the passion of new and vast developments to which they gave voice. Within "enlightened" circles the authority of Halacha diminished. The universal message of the prophets took firm root. Transformation evoked questions about the role of the rabbi, but anchors could not be abandoned without the search for new ones. Thus, questions were raised about the role of Reform rabbis.

These questions evoked a multitude of responses. Typical was the analysis offered by Rabbi Morton Berman in his address on *The Role of the Rabbi* (Jewish Institute of Religion, 1941) delivered at opening day exercises during the 20th anniversary of the Jewish Institute of Religion. From Jeremiah's words, "For instruction shall not perish from the priest, nor council from the wise, nor the word from the prophet" (18:18), Berman projected the classical schema for the Reform rabbinate.

He said the rabbi needed to combine the talents and authority of the priest, the prophet, and the sage. The problem was that the Reform rabbi could not rely on the traditional tools of command, admonition, and instruction. The efficacy of these traditions had diminished as a result of changes in the fabric and life of the Jewish community.

The priestly functions of command and directive were abandoned early in the evolution of Reform. The movement postured itself as antithetical to an absolute voice of authority, thus the priestly function gave way to the prophetic. We became a community of "ethical monotheists," not very different in significant ways from our non-Jewish brothers and sisters.

The realm of the rabbi as sage, based on the authority of the teacher, never diminished, but it, too, was reshaped. Secular expertise was given higher status than particularistic Jewish scholarship. Even 100 years after the Berlin *Culturverein*, sermons and lectures of rabbis who reflected on their role indicate that being expert in secular areas was perceived the means to securing rabbinic authority.

In a series of lectures at the HUC-JIR in Cincinnati in 1950, Rabbi Jacob J. Weinstein said:

> This is an age of specialization. The Rabbinate is, in fact, an *executive profession* (emphasis added). It partakes of many professional skills — psychiatrist, social worker, pedagogue, reformer, administrator. Since you cannot be proficient in all, you must become proficient in one.[1]

Weinstein's formulation of the rabbinic role reflected general wisdom at the time.

This was confirmed in a recently republished volume intended to serve as a guide to aspiring rabbis. In a chapter entitled "The Rabbi as a Teacher of Judaism: Priest, Prophet, or Sage?" Dr. Alfred Gottschalk wrote about the role of the rabbi.[2] He cited Rabbi Jacob Shankman's advice that the modern rabbi must at least be "a Jewish book-man familiar with the rich treasures of contemporary scholarly research, and even aspire to make one specific area of study and learning his own." Gottschalk added: "It is not uncommon to find in the Rabbinate men who have specialized in philosophy, sociology, family counseling, and a host of other intellectual and vocational interests, all of which they seek to integrate into their traditional calling and learning." The Reform rabbi speaks from a pulpit built from planks of secular and general learning.

There is yet another mission for which we are trained. "Because of the nature of American Jewish life, the Rabbi teaches not only his congregation but often is invited to speak to other groups about Judaism."[3] By this Gottschalk meant Christian congregations, campus student bodies, and Christian clergy.

This strong universalistic trend within Reform Judaism became suspect by the middle of the 20th century. By the time Morton Berman spoke in 1941, the tragedy in Europe was known. Jews appropriately questioned whether acceptance of non-traditional authorities was ever going to lead to full citizenship and acceptance.

We were challenged to examine again the sources of our authority as rabbis since we could not depend upon secular legitimization. We could not be valid as rabbis because we might be superb educators, political reformers, or organizers. Our authority was, and remains, Judaism, and "the Rabbi thus becomes the analyzer and the legitimizer of Jewish life."[4] More than that, the rabbi has *become* the message. Leo Baeck stated it eloquently: "The message is not the sermon of a preacher, but the man himself. ... The Rabbi must not deliver a message, he must deliver himself."[5]

Clearly, the Reform rabbinate has been reflective and self-judging. The rabbinate has considered its role, has investigated history, and has used it in order to envision the future. We have always been, and will continue to be, shaped by the dual forces of Reform Judaism and American society.

Our role in the next century is contingent upon the direction and power of these forces. The next generation of rabbis will be expected to meet the challenges of the same transforming pressures within American society and the Jewish community.

The confluence of these vectors causes us to turn our attention to the program of our seminary, which is responsible for training rabbis for future generations. A Task Force on Curriculum for the Hebrew Union College-Jewish Institute of Religion was directed

> to undertake a thorough study of the Rabbinic curriculum in light of the many changes that have occurred in our Rabbinic School, in our student body (e.g., women students, changing religious orientation-Reform background, attitudes toward ritual, etc.), ... in our lay constituency, and in the nature of the emerging ever more sophisticated Reform Jewish community.[6]

The administration of the College-Institute has recognized that our movement is in a transitional stage. The Reform movement will be different because our constituency and leadership is changing.

Since we can presume that rabbis will not be vastly different from our future lay leaders in life style and impressionability, the 1985 study by Winer, Seltzer, and Schwager, *Leaders of Reform Judaism*,[7] provides information about the future and can provide guidance in considering the future rabbinate.

Because there is an undeniable link between the role of the rabbi in the next century and the next generation of rabbis, let us consider the collective rabbinic portrait of the future.

An Americanized Rabbinate

The rabbis of the next century will be almost entirely without personal knowledge of their familial immigrant generation since the leaders of Reform Judaism are practically all native-born North Americans. Though there will be a continuing immigration from the Soviet Union, South America, and Israel, we do not foresee a vast wave of future immigration to the United States similar to that at the turn of the last century.

Most students who are entering the HUC-JIR are personally distant from the immigrant experience, the settlement houses, and the pervasive ethnicity that typified the immigrants to this country. Ethnic Judaism will not be available to them as the source of a firm identity.

The acculturation of the next generations of rabbis will also be reflected in their geographical diversity. Our future rabbis are growing up in a Jewish community that is a dispersed population in this country. They do not personally know the "feel" of Jewish neighborhoods. As a result, our future leaders are growing up to have greater familiarity with non-Jewish culture than with ethnic Jewry. East European and Sefardic influences will remain, but they will increasingly dissolve into the great wash of American life.

Raised, Educated, and Identified as Reform Jews

Increasing numbers of rabbis will be products of Reform Jewish households. Though they will be raised in homes affiliated with Reform synagogues, they may lack a deep knowledge of Reform Judaism. A conclusion stated by the Director of Admissions and Recruitment of HUC-JIR in *Profile of Entering Rabbinic Students* is that "a majority of students enter HUC with a limited vision of the Reform Movement in America. Very few have had an opportunity to experience the rich diversity of Reform Judaism."[8]

This would be expected as a result of the generational progression of Jews in this country. According to Steven Cohen, the greater the separation from the immigrant experience, the less likely one is to engage in ritual.

This analysis of the impact of generation upon Jewish identification points to how integration into modern society is a key to understanding broad changes in Jewish identification. Jews who are generationally close to the traditional heritage are most likely to express that closeness in concrete, ritual terms. As they integrate into society they may participate more extensively in formal institutions of the Jewish community even as their personal religiosity continues to decline.[9]

It can be expected that the rabbis of the next century will know little about the traditions of Judaism from their own upbringing. What they will learn and then practice ritually will develop from their study at the seminary. In both form and content Reform Judaism for the future rabbinate will begin with study and then develop into personal practice. If the next generation of rabbis matures in homes devoid of ritual, we can expect that, in some fashion, this will have an impact upon attitudes toward ritual.

A Varied Rabbinical Community

Cohen writes:

> The American Jewish family has been changing both in line with trends in the larger American family and in line with the influence exerted by a historical dynamic peculiar to American Jews. ... These trends mean increases in Jewish singles, childless, intermarrieds, and divorcees (or "alternative households").[10]

The rabbinic community of the next century will obviously be increasingly diverse in life situation and style:

1. More rabbis will be married to individuals who were not born as Jews. There will probably also be an increase in the number of rabbis not married to Jewish partners at the time of marriage.
2. The number of rabbis who themselves are Jews by choice will increase.
3. We can foresee an increase in the number of rabbis who, as a matter of choice, will not be married and who, therefore, will not have children.
4. There will be an increase in the number of gay and lesbian rabbis if sexual lifestyles are not considered a factor for admission to the HUC-JIR.
5. More individuals will enter the rabbinate as a second career. The size of the applicant pool for the College-Institute has already become a matter of great concern. HUC-JIR may be experiencing a decline in the number of qualified applicants, particularly men. Because of a concurrent increase in the number of available rabbinic opportunities, there may be a shortage of rabbis.

Without altering the standards for admission to the College-Institute, there will continue to be fewer graduates than available positions, especially if we consider the rabbinate outside the congregational world.

If the principle of supply and demand makes the rabbinate an attractive and stable profession, we may discover that individuals will naturally consider the rabbinate after having studied for, and being involved in, other professions. This would result in a rise in the median age of newly ordained rabbis.

The Impact of Women in the Rabbinate

The greatest change in the rabbinate in the past half century has been the ordination of women. Less than 20 years have passed since the first woman was ordained, and the impact has been remarkable.

It would be deceptive to view the change in the number of women in the rabbinate, which will undoubtedly continue to increase in the Conference, merely as a statistical factor. We are looking to the point when we will reach parity in the number of men and women in the Reform rabbinate.

The real impact of women in the rabbinate, though, goes beyond statistics. The nature of the rabbinate has already been altered in profound ways. The changing role of the rabbi, which will be discussed later, is directly related to its feminization. The entrance of women into the rabbinic work force has had profound effects in altering perceptions, creating more diverse models for rabbinic service, and generally changing our approach to the place of the rabbi in the community.

The composition of the CCAR will be greatly varied in the next century. Reform rabbis will emerge from backgrounds, lifestyles, and situations of great diversity, making the future Reform rabbinate very different from the rabbinic population of the past century. The composition of our rabbinic community will reflect the profound changes occurring within the Jewish community, which itself reflects the vast transformation occurring within society.

The rabbinate will be a far more heterogeneous community than ever before. It will have less access to the ethnic anchors of the past, and will need to lay claim to new modes of understanding, communication, and consensus. In addition, we will be a professional body that may experience a generation gap in a fashion different from that which the immigrant generation and its children experienced when they confronted the realities of the American society. We may be divorced from the personal apprenticeship and authentic home ritual training and experience of the type being sought by our constituency.

With some understanding of the population of the rabbinate in the next century, we can turn to the changing role of the rabbi.

The Changing Professional Role

Professional development was a primary interest of the 1985 Task Force on the Curriculum of the HUC-JIR. According to its preliminary report, there was almost unanimous concern about the training of rabbis as professionals, stemming from perceived lapses in the curriculum.

Professional development would not have been the primary concern of our colleagues a century ago. Rabbis were not trained to be counselors, educators, or administrators. If they functioned as such, it was by virtue of normal participation in the life of the community. The rabbinic role was not traditionally compartmentalized.

Modernity has had the effect of creating specialization. The change is a root cause for the identity conflict in the HUC-JIR. The dilemma is simply phrased: Is HUC-JIR a professional school or an academy of graduate Jewish studies? The question is directly related to the ambivalence within the rabbinate itself as to its ultimate priority.

There is reason to predict that in the future there will be a significant shift both in the perception and in the reality of the rabbi's role. Future generations of Jews will need, expect, and demand a thorough and deep knowledge of Judaism from their rabbis and will want rabbis to be able to apply that knowledge to life circumstances and situations. The rabbi's professional role then will have no general or particular secular significance.

This clearly mandates a subtle change in the educational priorities of the College-Institute. Professional development will have merit only as it provides the rabbi with comfort to function in a varied range of situations. Clearly, the primary aim will be to educate our students to apply Judaism to the complex and diverse circumstances that Jews confront.

Our roles as counselors, educators, administrators, programmers, facilitators, and the like will have little meaning apart from this single overriding mission. Congregants seeking rabbis for counsel, will do so in order to know how Jewish wisdom is applicable to their problem. The rabbis' role as programmers will not be to attract Jews with novelty or secular relevance. The purpose of the synagogue program will be to deepen Jewish knowledge, understanding, and sensitivities.

Where prophetic pronouncements and universalism once defined the rabbinic role, in the next century, it will be the specific and particular values of Jewish learning that will mark the value of the rabbi. This clearly implies a narrowing of concern, which has most dramatically been observed in the political arena. The traditional perception of Jews as political liberals still continues, but with qualification. In *The Political Future of American Jews*[11] Earl Raab and Seymour Martin Lipset, gave an explanation for the political mood of American Jews: "In this display of opinions on social welfare, Jews represent a disproportionate *supportive audience* rather than a political association." Yet, "with respect to the kind of integrated activism which has made the Jewish political association influential, observers have noted a trend of ominous 'narrowing' within Jewish life."[12]

Steven Cohen outlined three sorts of constraints on Jewish political liberalism, including (1) a *traditional subculture* that "frowns upon liberal causes to many social issues"; (2) a concern for Jewish self-interests that "militates against a universalist outlook in political affairs"; and (3) assimilation that tends to make Jews more conservative.[13]

As Jews tend to withdraw from universal agendas and begin to raise self-concern to a priority, they will desire and demand to know the relevance and application of their faith, history, and traditions to increasingly complicated issues. These new circumstances, including development within the consciousness of the Jewish community, will demand of rabbis that they continuously engage in the traditional mission of learning for the purpose of staying current and alert to their responsibility. Where rabbis once needed to help their fellow Jews face a hostile and confusing external world, rabbis in the future will help Jews understand and deal with a confusing and complex internal world. Jews will need support in dealing with issues of personal meaning, spiritualism, finitude, and their relationship with God, along with issues of social justice.

Jewish knowledge will be sought in order to apply it to an increasingly broad range of issues, and rabbis will be needed to make that happen. The Jewish community will want rabbis available for that purpose at all levels throughout the Jewish institutional world. As a result, rabbis will be in demand to participate in a host of new professional and organizational environments presently not filled by ordained clergy.

The process has already begun. Rabbis are being invited to apply for positions which never before were viewed as rabbinic vocations. Chaplaincies in hospitals, universities, prisons, and elder-care centers, as well as positions as college teachers are some of the employment openings for which rabbis are being sought in increasing numbers. Jewish community centers in the larger cities are hiring rabbis on staff to be responsible for Jewish content in programming. Bureaus of Jewish Education will increasingly involve rabbis in key positions for developing curricula and programs for teacher training. Social welfare organizations and social service agencies are seeking more rabbinic involvement for other areas, not just for counseling. We will be needed to translate more fully the "Jewish" aspect of our organizations' mission into actuality.

Along with the increase of diversified rabbinic placements will come a tendency toward specialization. This will accelerate a movement away from seeing the rabbi as a super professional in congregational life. Rabbis will be more expert in applying their knowledge to very specific tasks, and in each area the demand will be for the rabbi to teach, to explain, and to augment Jewish learning.

In conclusion, we foresee parallel trends toward greater rabbinic placement and increased specialization. As each organization seeks rabbinic involvement, the opportunity for rabbis to work intensively and selectively with specific functions within the community will increase. The congregational rabbi will be expert in the central themes of congregational life without directing its administrative aspects. Except for geographical areas with small Jewish density, the individual rabbi will not serve as a resource to a broad expanse of Jewish institutions, organizations, hospitals, and universities. These agencies will hire individual rabbis to serve their own particular needs.

Emphasizing the Faith Aspect

The Jewish community of the next century will be altered by virtue of demography and history. Almost all Reform Jewish leaders have been born in North America and — except for larger cities, where immigration from the Soviet Union may have an impact on the Jewish environment — the immigrant generation is disappearing. Short of a global catastrophe resulting in another wave of immigration, the American Jewish community will be insulated against massive cultural impacts.

In an ethnic sense, what we have become is what we will continue to be. The flavor of our community will not be altered significantly, except that we will be increasingly acculturated. Eastern European traditions as a dominant Jewish cultural expression will continue to dissipate. Fewer and fewer families will have a working knowledge of Yiddish; Jewish foods will be remembered with nostalgia and recipes will be forgotten; the flavor of distinctly Jewish neighborhoods and communities will all but disappear.

Although Jews may continue to live together in the same communities, nothing distinctive about the physical or cultural aspects of these communities will define them except institutionality.

As the ethnic definition of Judaism recedes, ideology, faith, covenant, and belief will become more significant. Jews will increasingly view themselves as members of a religious, rather than a cultural, community. A concept of "peoplehood" will continue to be binding, but the language of peoplehood will have an increasingly spiritual tone.

Rabbis will need to talk about God in absolutely clear terms. The spiritual development of the rabbi, both prior to and during rabbinic training, will be essential groundwork for continuing spiritual development during the period of rabbinic service.

More Jews, and in greater frequency, will want their rabbi to explain the meaning of life's vicissitudes. Prayer will become the primary focus of worship, and the success of prayer will become the measure of the worship experience. While many would argue that prayer has always been the primary focus of worship, a good case can be made that a personal prayer experience within community worship has not been the aim of Reform worship.

We can find an indication of the present purpose of worship by analyzing the manner in which rabbis prepare. At present the rabbi, as leader of worship, functions as director/producer of a smooth, unified endeavor. A rabbi's preparation for a worship service generally consists of writing and preparing a sermon for verbal delivery and/or arrangements for a guest speaker or program; organizing the order and cues for individuals participating in the service (i.e., cantor, music director, musicians, other rabbis, representatives of the congregation); preparing relevant certificates for life-cycle events occurring at services, along with the coordination of those participating in these rites; selecting the services from *Gates of Prayer* and preparing for the reading of the Torah.

Rabbinic preparation emphasizes the passive posture of the congregation in the worship service. Prayer, and preparation for it, occupies a supporting and secondary role, if at all.

If the spiritual and prayer needs of the congregation increase, then the worship service will increasingly become the focus of these needs. The rabbi's role will change accordingly and will focus on the preparation of an environment for prayer. The rabbi's own desire, ability, and willingness to pray will be immeasurably significant. Sermons, in their present form, will probably not be relevant, and we can expect the teaching of Torah in alternative forms to succeed better. Congregants will expect to be taught Torah for specific and immediate application and to comprehend the role of commentaries in the explication and expansion of text. Jews will want an intimate relationship with the textual sources of their identity, and rabbis will have to help them accomplish this.

Teaching during the worship service will be less directed toward motivating broad social movements, and, instead, concentrate upon helping the individual discover personal religious significance. Congregants will aggressively focus on issues of belief, spiritual development, and the values of Judaism as they apply to the common, and sometimes mundane, elements of daily life.

Divorced from authentic ethnic roots, study by candidates for conversion will be centered upon theological issues. We can expect that there will be substantial discussion of *mitzvah* and its meaning, of covenant, and of each candidate's personal responsibility as a member of the Jewish people.

Rabbinic training will have, as a foremost goal, the cultivation of each rabbi's ability to learn, discuss, and teach, so that each individual will be able to seek a personal and collective relationship with God in an authentic manner.

Ritual Life of the Community

The present move toward a deepening spiritual and religious identity will profoundly affect the role of the rabbi in both the congregational and non-congregational realms. We have already witnessed an intensification of ritual celebration. According to the study by Steven Cohen,

> Generation has diverse and, at times, offsetting and non-linear relationships with various dimensions of Jewish identity. Thus the advance of generation brought both the erosion of certain "traditional" ritual practices and the stabilization in the practice of more "modern" observances.[14]

The need for ritual observances as a framework for one's life has not lessened, while particular "traditions" have not been adequate as a response to that need. People may therefore be less "traditional" and yet more involved with redefined or newly created religious practices.

These may appear to be opposite trends. On the one hand, acculturation continues and accelerates among certain segments of our population; on the other hand, assimilation is less current. Young Jews who yearn to live their lives within the American scene are also comfortable with their Jewish identities. They live in the mainstream of American society with acceptance and pride in Jewish selfhood. They have learned from the Nazi era and from the Soviet Union that assimilation does not buy acceptance.

We have also become witnesses to the proliferation of conservative and fundamentalist movements in our time. We have watched the shameless use of power by religious parties devoid of self-recrimination or shame.

Furthermore, we have seen our own American constitutional democracy sanction religious expression in politics, in the classroom, and in all forms of media. Some political candidates talk proudly and openly about their religious connections. Some have been funded and supported by missionizing religious groups. Ministers have waged legitimate presidential campaigns. We are a society that is willing to tolerate public demonstrations of religious identity. It is "in" to be religious in public.

In this context, then, Marrano behavior is clearly nonproductive. Hiding as a Jew will foster neither success nor acceptance. If public expressions of Christianity do not prevent a climb to power and authority, then the same should be true for public expressions of Judaism. There is no merit in believing that ritual, as a public portrayal of identity, prevents a mainstream existence. Thus, the doors swing open to public ritual practice.

There are other factors that will result in an increase of ritual involvement. Feminist spokespersons say that we are coming to the end of an era in which "body" and "spirit" are treated as separate and compartmentalized. They say we need to move toward greater "embodiment," which is described as the unification of body, soul, mind, and feeling into a single act. This approach to the person as an integral whole is directly relevant to ritual and prayer. It calls for a total physical involvement in the rhythm of prayer.

When American Christian worship became the model for Jewish worship, unity and control pervaded our ritual. Reform worship had the effect of leveling and equalizing the worship experience. All individuals prayed at the same rate, in the same way, in the same order, and with the same public intensity. The particularistic expressions of Jewish celebration were doomed. A critique of the Reform movement is its ritual frigidity. We pray without the body involvement that is so much a part of traditional worship.

There has been some change in the last decades. Public manifestations of Judaism inside and outside one's house are more pronounced, and there apparently is greater comfort with Jewish symbols. We are becoming more closely identified, and we are expressing that identity in a variety of ways.

We will continue to redefine ritual in less "traditional" language. We will consider personal and individual ritual from the perspective of our need to celebrate all of life's changes. We have already heard calls for liturgies and rituals to signify major events heretofore not noted through Reform ritual acts. A Reform ritual for divorce is needed. Some have suggested ritual expressions at a time of miscarriage or at the onset of menstruation or menopause. There may need to be a ritual voice for the horror and helplessness of victims of violent crimes.

Clearly, the suggestion is that there are profound events, many of which are quite naturally part of life, that need to be "celebrated." The occasion of the first departure for college is a significant time for both child and parents. It can be celebrated, as should be the time of a first employment, or the loss of employment. Ritual note should be taken of the youngest child leaving home, the birth of a grandchild, serious illness, or imminent death. These moments, which had traditional responses, still demand a meaningful ritual in our movement.

Rabbis cannot be involved as leaders in the plethora of these rituals. Rather, they will become the teachers and expeditors of ritual, helping Reform Jews become familiar with ritual as a proper response to significant rites of passage.

Rabbis will need to acquaint individuals with the possibility of satisfactory ritual expression in old and new forms. Rabbis will need to be thoroughly acquainted, and at ease, with ritual observance and traditions, and they will need to know, teach, and talk about them.

Our constituents are searching for traditional modes and directions. They want to know which rituals will work for them, and how to practice them properly. They perceive ritual as a linkage, as an act of continuity. They desire to make knowledgeable choices.

This is an area that has been singled out by the Task Force on the Curriculum of the HUC-JIR. Its draft states:

> Students need a step-by-step survey of the rituals and procedures associated with the total life cycle and yearly festival cycle. ... The goal of such exposure should be to familiarize students with commonly accepted procedures and significant variations of them so that students may have a sound basis for formulating their own patterns of procedure and practice.[15]

Clearly, the area of ritual will be a major component of rabbinic function in the next century.

The Rabbi as Respondent

An engaging role in which the rabbi of the next century will be involved is the traditional area of responsa. There has always been something very practical, elucidating, and noble about this form of interchange through which individuals and communities sought the wisdom and guidance of authoritative rabbis. At times, the questions were purely legal; at other times the issues were simple, practical matters that emerged from everyday life.

The questions raised in the next century will expand into complex areas including, but not limited to, ethical issues created by advanced technology. In every professional and scientific field there are pressing dilemmas demanding responses based on textual and interpretative substance.

Consider the issues raised by technological advances in the field of reproduction and birth. The available techniques of genetic engineering raise questions about the fundamentals of creation and about our right to be involved in altering it. How much can one tamper with the genetic pool for the sake of preventing diseases, and how much to improve the qualities of a family line? How does one create models for sorting out the issues? Is there a difference between genetic manipulation within the same cell and the transplanting of genes from other organisms? How much change in genetic structure should be allowed, and how much is appropriate to preclude in altering basic genetic definition?

We are confronting ethical issues beyond the field of reproduction and birth. Does the improvement of human health allow for animal experimentation — under what conditions, to what extent, and under whose stewardship? Is surrogate parenting legitimate? What are the rights of the birth parents in cases of adoption? What are the rights of the child to know ancestry?

The allotment of medical resources is a continuing dilemma. Scientists are asking whether it is proper to utilize the results of Nazi experiments performed on humans for contemporary lifesaving research.

We are also concerned about the treatment of patients who have contracted diseases of which we do not know the infection mechanism. How should these people be treated? Is quarantine appropriate for the protection of society? How do we balance the rights of the individual with the rights of society? Available medical and scientific material indicates that the incredible rate of technological advances makes it impossible to make predictions even about the next 20 years. We can be certain, however, that the future will raise a host of ethical issues.

Every profession is facing previously uncharted ethical areas. Lawyers are seeking guidance about the use of evidence gathered in immoral ways for the sake of very moral ends. Some of the recent cases in which Jews have been involved in illegal business dealings raised serious questions regarding the moral values that are inherent in the institutions of Jewish life, including, but not limited to, the synagogue.

Future ethical questions will emanate from familial arrangements as well as from interpersonal quandaries. There will be issues that will impinge on the behavior of each individual, who will look to the rabbi for guidance.

Ethical scrutiny in the next century will mandate the rabbi's comfort in applying pertinent texts to these issues. It is inconceivable that the individual rabbi would be called upon to adjudicate the full range of ethical dilemmas, but it is certain that each rabbi will need to apply Judaism to the questions that are being raised. Demands on rabbis to give guidance and direction, whether independently or within the context of ethics committees, will become central.

The pragmatic impact of ethical questioning and Jewish response will be especially great because of a historical Reform tendency toward independent decision. Moral anarchy and situational ethics have not satisfactorily met the needs of people who are in search of timeless and steady anchors. The treasured teachings of Judaism will become a crucial area to which Jews will look for guidance. It will be essential for the rabbi to know how to use, organize, and apply the full range of traditional texts for responsa purposes.

Our institutions will also occupy crucial roles in providing responsa. The use of the CCAR's Committee on Responsa, as well as the newly established Committee on Ethics of the UAHC, will grow in scope and import. We can predict that increased organizational support for the work of these committees will result in the convocation of conferences and task forces in order to handle the full range of ethical issues that we are only now beginning to comprehend.

Re-evaluating the *Tzedaka* Role

We are discovering that the needs of the past which gave birth to certain community functions may be rather constant. As we look for models, the *kehila*, as a community structure, may provide lessons and direction. That is not to say that the community will re-create itself in a form that is centuries old, but it does mean that we will need to consider traditional forms for their possible future significance. The authority of the community as a whole will gain as a collective force and conscience.

This will become especially significant in the issues typically identified as "social welfare" in the broadest sense. As our government has withdrawn support from many programs that have benefited those on the fringes of society, a deep void has been created. Jewish organizations, agencies, and synagogues have begun to address those apparent and critical needs that were previously met by government.

Some of the problems are most keenly felt in the Jewish community and some of the solutions are already structured. Factors of transiency, mobility, and family dissolution have a severe impact on the health and well-being of Judaism and the Jewish community. The problems call for a creative, significant, and forceful role of our institutions. The establishment of *chavurot* has been one solution helping individuals who have moved away from their family of origin to connect with "artificial" extended families. But it has not been enough. Much more needs to be done, and it presents a major challenge for the Reform Jewish community of the next century. The use of social workers within synagogues, the formation of self-help groups (e.g., single parents, children of divorce, widows/widowers, unmarried singles, never-married singles) signals the crisis we are confronting and our response to it.

Jews will increasingly look to the synagogue and to other agencies of Jewish life for help. Whether these individuals will be affiliated with Jewish institutional life is not the question, for it may happen that affiliation, as we know it, will not be the credential by which our communities determine their responsibilities and commitments.

The tendency toward greater particularism and identity will not prevent us from responding to the universalistic call of responsibility to all peoples. The synagogue and other Jewish agencies will increasingly network with all religious institutions to provide critical help to the non-Jewish community.

Programs for the homeless, the poor, the alienated and the alien, minorities, migrant workers, refugees, mentally and physically handicapped — all will increase in scope and dimension and will be funded and supported by the agencies of Jewish life, independently or together with other religious organizations. The rabbi's role in the area of creative *tzedaka* and *gemilut chasadim* will be essential. Not only will rabbis be called upon to provide vision; they will also be involved in particular programmatic ways. Part of our training will have to be that of community organization.

Rabbis will be actively involved as Federation executives. The perceived tension between synagogues and the general community fund-raising campaigns will be less significant in the future as lines of cooperation will replace lines of battle. We are learning that when one Jewish institution succeeds, all succeed. Past tension and competition will give way to a new symbiotic and mutually advantageous relationship, in which synagogues are funded by Federation campaigns for which they will be active fundraisers.

Since the training of rabbis will have a global disposition, we can expect that rabbis will be best suited to bring about a natural merging of purpose. As rabbis take part in the administration of Jewish agencies other than synagogues, we can expect heightened community cooperation together with a continued appreciation for the specific purpose of each constituent organization.

Unity within communities will augment the pooling of resources for financial and programmatic efficiency. We can foresee joint educational programming. Academies of adult Jewish study will be supported as a broad-based community effort. Conversion programs and trips to Israel will be community ventures. Rabbis will be the natural professionals to run these programs.

Mutual cooperation will eventually alter our physical facilities. Although there are already community campuses in some parts of the country, we can expect an expansion of this concept. It is sensible to house a variety of Jewish organizations in the same physical facility, especially if they are engaged in common purpose and directed toward cooperative unity.

Along with the programmatic and physical manifestations of cooperative community engagement, we will need to provide specialized help for Jews, as historically practiced. Let us consider that it is again necessary to organize in every Jewish community a *Chevra Kadisha*, a *Bikur Cholim* society, and a host of other helping organizations as fulfillment of *mitzvot*. The Jewish population of an area will be treated as *community affiliated* rather than as organizationally affiliated.

The rabbi will be essential to fostering this concept and in arranging a systematic structural response. Since the rabbinic charge is to serve all Israel, the rabbi will be an appropriate leader within this restructured Jewish community. By virtue of training, institutional parochialism would not be a limiting factor.

Feminization of the Rabbinate

We cannot overlook the profound change that the inclusion of women in the rabbinate has effected. Nor can we fully predict the manner in which the profession will change as a result of an increase in the percentage of women within the membership and the leadership of the CCAR.

Certainly, the impact of women is far beyond their being role models for our youngsters and beyond the demand for nonsexist liturgical language. Very little today has not been affected by the women's movement.

Ritual and worship are significantly influenced by the unique perspective and input of women. The confluence of spiritual and physical language, already discussed, will continue to shape our approach to the worship experience. The notion of the rabbinate as a helping profession has been redefined as a result of having women in the profession.

What about the future? Initially we might imagine that the definition of success will change as a result of women in the rabbinate. There is reason to believe that the typical movement of rabbis from smaller to larger congregations, or (as is typically described) to more "prestigious" congregations, will be re-examined.

There is already a tendency among our students to consider shared careers and family responsibility. Some recent graduates have sought part-time positions, or positions that will allow more private time, affording them the opportunity to stay home with children. If this trend continues, especially with two-career families, we might find that lifestyle will be a high priority in career decision. Smaller congregations may become attractive because they would allow parenting to coexist with career. Noncongregational positions will also become increasingly attractive by reason of specialization and of work situation.

Just as the definition of success in the rabbinate may be recast, so may be the definition of career or of "full-time" jobs. It may become more common for rabbis to take a leave of absence during their careers. Part-time positions may be in greater demand because of scheduling benefits, and it may become common for rabbis to take time away from employment during the child-rearing years.

Alternatively, full-time positions may be recast as 37-40-hour jobs. Rabbis typically pride themselves on dedicating the time necessary to complete tasks without regard to the hours spent; they often work 60-70, even 80 hours a week. It is obviously impossible to be involved in the life and schedule of children when working these hours.

Rabbis who have children, or who are intent upon spending substantial time with a spouse, will face the decision of either working part-time (20 hours a week), taking time away from careers, or demanding that a full-time rabbinic position be viewed within the 40-hour work week framework.

Our movement will be confronted with the need to accept limitations on the time demands imposed upon rabbis or we will have an increasing contingent of rabbis forsaking full-time positions (over 40 hours a week) in order to raise children.

If the rabbi's position is allowed to have time limitations, we will have a better chance of keeping our Reform rabbis in the congregational workplace.

It certainly can be argued that none of these changes is intrinsically linked to women in the rabbinate, but there is clear indication that sensitivity to family life and the coordination of career and family demands have become more pronounced since women have entered the rabbinate.

Technology

One cannot consider the future without taking account of the impact of technological advances. Certain ethical questions already discussed are a direct result of these advances. We have not been able to adjust our ethical and structural systems to keep pace with the rate of technological advancement.

Technology will also have an impact upon our workplace. There are data-base systems utilized by synagogues that keep information about members immediately available. The interest, talents, and involvement of every member can be tracked. This enables the leadership of the congregation to know of each member's history — for example, how often the congregant has been personally invited to participate and what his or her record of response has been. If the systems are used correctly, noninvolvement will not be a result of oversight.

Technology will also expand the available means of communication between institutions and their constituents. Some congregations are already dependent on television and radio broadcasts to air worship services. Video- and audio-tapes and closed-circuit television are used in religious schools and for general programs.

The greatest benefit in the future will be to those who are physically unable to come to our buildings. We will need to redefine the meaning of participation, which presently implies attendance. We will be able to serve the aged, the disabled, and the ill who cannot travel. The newest applied technology allows homebound members to listen by telephone to events taking place in the synagogue. The system allows an individual to listen to religious services, life-cycle events, and other programs by accessing designated lines. It also enables people who are out of town to listen in on life-cycle events.

We will redefine the centrality of our institutional facilities. Consider, for instance, that it may be possible for Jews to study,

attend meetings and worship services, and receive information and
communications even if they cannot come to the building.

The role of the rabbi will not change radically in content, but
the forms of rabbinic interaction will change. It will be important
that rabbis understand the new technology and its possible
applications for achieving established goals. Authenticity and reli-
ability continue to be the cornerstones of rabbinic function and
acceptance, but more options will be available to rabbis for the
expression of concern, teaching, and fulfilling the mission which
they have established for themselves.

The Rabbi as Student

The authority of the rabbi depends on the mastery of information, text, and tradition. We can expect that the traditional focus
of the rabbi will be clearer and sharper than in the past. Rabbis
will be expected to speak with profound expertise and explicit par-
ticularity from the sources of rabbinic authority.

The application of Torah to specific issues will be essential and
will be sought increasingly. Eloquent statements of universal
teaching will always have a role in shaping vision, but Jews will
want to know what is behind that vision and what Jewish guidelines apply to it.

The rabbi will need to be engaged in constant renewal and
study. The test of rabbinic skill will be in the ability of the individual rabbi to teach and guide according to traditional text,
learning, and wisdom. Rabbis will need to excel as spokespersons
for ethical direction emanating from the consideration and evaluation of past Jewish messages, and by doing so, will add another
level to the evolution of Jewish understanding.

The next century will be one in which rabbinic functions will
reflect an expansion and renovation of traditional forms. We will
emphasize what has already served us well, following models
conceived in past centuries. Therein lies the irony. With vast and
sweeping transformations, the rabbinate will utilize traditional
forms with great ease. We will no more be bound by past decisions than we are now, but we will be expected to know those
specific decisions and to derive positions by re-evaluating them.

In many ways the Jewish community is in a transitional stage.
The Reform movement is already different from what it was a
century ago. The pace of change within the movement has quick-
ened, yet, as tumultuous as the next decades may be, we will call
on the sources of our authority with greater vigor and commitment. The vast repository of Jewish text, knowledge, wisdom,
and understanding is our possession. It is sound, permanent, and

evolving. It provides a balance when all else seems elusive and transient. The voice of the rabbi will be heeded as long as it remains absolutely fixed to the source of authority which gives us the right to speak. It is *that* which Jews will want to hear and which provides us with a particular and special perspective.

Jews will want to know what it means to be a Jew. They will want to understand the substance of their identity. Rabbis will need to study continuously both for their own renewal and in order to answer questions never before asked.

The Rabbi and Israel

The State of Israel is at a point of transition. It is facing critical external challenges, but it is also confronting challenges of meaning from within. The Reform movement and its treatment by Israel will be a mirror of the quality of Israel as a "Jewish" state.

As a result of our First Year in Israel Program, many ordinees consider *aliya*. As a result of significant changes made in the structure, policy, and representation of the Jewish Agency and the World Zionist Congress, Reform Judaism as an ideology and as a movement in Israel is beginning to make headway.

We would expect that there will be a tremendous role for the Reform movement in the State of Israel. Yet the leadership of that movement may need individuals who are native Israelis. The expansion of our rabbinic program in Jerusalem, allowing for Israelis to become Reform rabbis, is a most important factor in bringing about major change within the Israeli population. Our movement will depend on sabras to speak authentically on our behalf.

We will begin to see an increasing contingent of Israeli Reform rabbis in Israel as our movement grows in the Jewish State. Jewish contacts between Israel and the United States will remain strong despite strains upon that relationship.

Our Relationship with Other Jews

There are deep tensions between our movement and other streams of Judaism in the American community. We have been cursed, insulted, and debased by those who consider Reform Judaism a heresy. The question has been asked once again: Will there continue to be one Jewish people?

History tells us that this question is part of any change or evolution within our community. Certainly, there will be one Jewish people. But we need to intensify our efforts to bring about common purpose and programs. No one gains by the internecine battles raging among Jewish institutions. There will need to be discussion and rapprochement. Our representative rabbinical organizations will have to find a way to coexist even if we do not find a way to agree.

Diversity has been the key to our survival. We will always have a multitude of positions and voices. In some ways it makes us healthy. The next century will be one of greater extremism and of greater accord. We will not be able to obliterate the point of view of those who are fanatic in their adherence to their "truth." However, the community will move in the direction of greater cooperation and understanding, for therein lies the road to survival.

Conclusion

The Reform rabbinate is on the threshold of an era in which many of our visions may materialize. We are entering the second century of our existence as a Conference of Reform rabbis. We will continue to be innovative and courageous in our roles. We will be called upon to fulfill classic roles in extremely creative ways.

Our basic mission has not changed, but the environment has. Jews still want to be Jews. They need to be certain and clear about their identity. Members of our congregations will call upon us to help them comprehend the source of their religious being and to help them apply the content of their tradition to new and pressing situations.

Our mission is, perhaps, more clearly in focus now than in past decades. Our direction is more precise; our authority more firmly connected to its roots; our place as teachers of Torah more firmly established. The Jewish community will seek us and need us to speak with strong voices. We will demand of ourselves full comprehension of our essential role in ensuring the survival of our communities and in improving the quality of their Jewish life in the next century. There is good reason for us to anticipate the coming years with enthusiasm and excitement. Our community is vital, as is the Reform rabbinate. We move on with conviction, dedication, and enthusiasm.

NOTES

[1] "The Rabbi as Preacher, Pastor and Community Worker," Chicago: KAM Temple, 1950.

[2] Alfred Gottschalk, *To Learn and to Teach: Your Life as a Rabbi* (New York: Rosen Publishing Group, 1988), p. 25.

[3] *Ibid.*

[4] Berman, *The Role of the Rabbi*, p. 15.

[5] Leo Baeck, "Predigt und Wahrheit," 1928, reprinted in *Wege im Judentum* (Berlin: 1933), p. 311.

[6] *Innovators of Torah* (Cincinnati: Hebrew Union College, 1988), p. 1.

[7] New York, UAHC, 1987.

[8] Gary Zola, *Profile of Entering Rabbinic Students* (Cincinnati: Hebrew Union College, 1988), p. 1.

[9] *American Modernity and Jewish Identity* (New York: Tavistock Publications, 1983), p. 74.

[10] *Ibid.*, p. 173.

[11] New York, American Jewish Congress, 1985.

[12] P. 19.

[13] *American Modernity*, p. 151.

[14] *Ibid.*, p. 172.

[15] *Innovators of Torah,* p. 44.